Comments on other *Amazing Stories* from readers & reviewers

"Tightly written volumes filled with lots of wit and humour about famous and infamous Canadians."
Eric Shackleton, *The Globe and Mail*

"The heightened sense of drama and intrigue, combined with a good dose of human interest is what sets Amazing Stories *apart."*
Pamela Klaffke, *Calgary Herald*

"This is popular history as it should be... For this price, buy two and give one to a friend."
Terry Cook, a reader from Ottawa, on **Rebel Women**

"Glasner creates the moment of the explosion itself in graphic detail...she builds detail upon gruesome detail to create a convincingly authentic picture."
Peggy McKinnon, *The Sunday Herald,* on **The Halifax Explosion**

"It was wonderful...I found I could not put it down. I was sorry when it was completed."
Dorothy F. from Manitoba on **Marie-Anne Lagimodière**

"Stories are rich in description, and bristle with a clever, stylish realness."
Mark Weber, *Central Alberta Advisor,* on **Ghost Town Stories II**

"A compelling read. Bertin...has selected only the most intriguing tales, which she narrates with a wealth of detail."
Joyce Glasner, *New Brunswick Reader,* on **Strange Events**

"The resulting book is one readers will want to share with all the women in their lives."
Lynn Martel, *Rocky Mountain Outlook,* on **Women Explorers**

SECRETS OF LAKE SIMCOE

AMAZING STORIES®

SECRETS OF LAKE SIMCOE

Fascinating Stories from Ontario's past

Andrew Hind
and Maria da Silva

HISTORY

James Lorimer & Company Ltd., Publishers
Toronto

James Lorimer & Company Ltd., Publishers acknowledges the support of the Ontario Arts Council. We acknowledge the financial support of the Government of Canada through the Canada Book Fund for our publishing activities. We acknowledge the support of the Canada Council for the Arts for our publishing program. We acknowledge the Government of Ontario through the Ontario Media Development Corporation's Ontario Book Initiative.

ONTARIO ARTS COUNCIL
CONSEIL DES ARTS DE L'ONTARIO

Canada Council
for the Arts

Library and Archives Canada Cataloguing in Publication

Hind, Andrew
Secrets of Lake Simcoe / Andrew Hind, Maria da Silva.

(Amazing stories)
Includes index.
Issued also in electronic format.
ISBN 978-1-55277-577-6

1. Simcoe, Lake (Ont.)—History. 2. Simcoe, Lake, Region (Ont.)—History.
I. Da Silva, Maria II. Title. III. Series: Amazing stories (Toronto, Ont.)

FC3095.L345H46 2010   971.3'17   C2010-902651-9

James Lorimer & Company Ltd., Publishers
317 Adelaide Street West, Suite 1002
Toronto, ON, Canada
M5V 1P9
www.lorimer.ca

Printed and bound in Canada

FSC
Mixed Sources
Product group from well-managed
forests, controlled sources and
recycled wood or fiber

Cert no. SW-COC-001271
www.fsc.org
©1996 Forest Stewardship Council

This book is dedicated to the Sibbald family
of The Briars Resort.

Contents

Introduction

Even a quick look at a map of Ontario reveals one inescapable geographic reality: Lake Simcoe dominates the central part of the province. It's big—by far the largest body of water between Lake Ontario and Lake Huron—and it's located right in the heart of the province.

But not only does Lake Simcoe dominate the map, it dominates the history of central Ontario as well, and that's what *Secrets of Lake Simcoe* sets out to explore through a collection of fascinating and largely unknown stories. How many know that Lake Simcoe played a vital role in safeguarding Canada during the War of 1812, that explorer Sir John Franklin passed through it during one of his Arctic explorations, or that Ontario's original cottage country was located here rather than in Muskoka? Not many. It seems that the deep waters of Lake Simcoe guards its secrets well, as if jealously hoarding a precious treasure. And in a sense these stories are a treasure, as they tell much about Ontario's development.

At 48 kilometres (30 miles) long and 29 kilometres (18 miles) wide and with a maximum depth of 41 meters (136 feet), Lake Simcoe is huge. Some have likened it to a sixth Great Lake. It certainly qualifies, if not for its size then for its historic importance: for centuries, in the era when there were no roads and the landscape was covered with impenetrable forests, Lake Simcoe was the most important waterway in the province. It formed a vital link between Lakes Ontario and Huron, helping open up the north and the west for natives, fur traders, soldiers, explorers, settlers, and industrialists.

It's impossible to pinpoint when Lake Simcoe first began its rise to prominence. The lake played an important role in the lives of the Huron and Ojibwa natives who inhabited most of central Ontario and had done so for hundreds, likely thousands of years. The natives paddled its length in birchbark canoes while trading and conducting war, fished its depths to supplement their diets, and established settlements along its shores. The Huron called Lake Simcoe *Ouentaron*, or "the beautiful lake." To the Ojibwa it was *Wahweyagahmah*, "round lake." But whatever name they called it, to native peoples Lake Simcoe was an important element of their lifestyle.

Seventeen-year-old Etienne Brûlé was the first European to see Lake Simcoe when he was sent to scout the interior in 1610. Samuel de Champlain, the famed explorer, followed a few years later in 1615. But while several Jesuit missions were established in the area to convert natives to Christianity, and there may have been fur-trade forts as well, in general the French did little to develop or exploit Lake Simcoe (which they called *Lac aux Claies*, "lake of the fish weirs," in reference to the native fishing fences at the narrows between Lake

Introduction

Simcoe and Lake Couchiching) during the two centuries it was part of New France.

In 1763, at the end of the Seven Years War, Canada became a British possession and shortly after, Lake Simcoe became a hive of activity. Canoes and bateaux belonging to the North West Company, a fur trading enterprise, began to pass over the lake with ever-increasing frequency as the fur trade gathered momentum.

Then, in 1793, Lieutenant-Governor John Graves Simcoe saw the lake while surveying the province's interior and gave it its modern name. Though some believe Simcoe egotistically named the lake for himself, in actual fact it was intended to honor his father, Captain John Simcoe of the Royal Navy. Lieutenant-Governor Simcoe was preoccupied with the very real possibility of an American invasion of Canada and began building Yonge Street from York (present-day Toronto) to the shores of Lake Simcoe as the first leg of an overland route to Lake Huron following the old native/fur trader route. Simcoe knew that traffic along Lakes Ontario and Erie could easily be disrupted by enemy ships, severing British ties to the West, but an overland route through central Ontario was far more difficult to sever. The wisdom of Simcoe's preparations was revealed in 1812 when the United States declared war and invaded: during the conflict that followed, Yonge Street and Lake Simcoe played a pivotal role in keeping the country from falling into American hands.

After the War of 1812, settlement of Lake Simcoe's shores was not long in coming. Holland Landing, situated at the northern end of Yonge Street and with access to Lake Simcoe via the Holland River, became the gateway to the region and a thriving port community. From here, settlements slowly spread up the shores of the lake, and eventually further into the interior. For decades most traffic bound for or from the lake, whether it was people or goods, passed through this town. It was only with the arrival of rail lines in the 1850s that Holland Landing began to lose its position of prominence.

While most settlers were common folk from the British Isles, the government encouraged retired military officers to settle the region by offering free land grants as reward for their service to the Crown. It was believed they would assume administrative, political, and judicial leadership, and thereby form a solid foundation upon which society could develop. The plan worked; their rank and experiences brought respect, and the retired army and navy officers became the gentry for this region. In many cases, they built elaborate manor homes that wouldn't have looked out of place in the British countryside (some of which still stand today), and furnished them with treasures brought over from the old country. These homes and the people residing within them became islands of culture and refinement in a frontier region.

Governor Sir Peregrine Maitland envisioned great

things in store for Lake Simcoe. Centrally located, the hub of Ontario's water transportation system and yet far from the reach of any invading American army, Maitland reasoned that Lake Simcoe would make an ideal location for the province's capital. He would move the capital from York, which had proven itself vulnerable to attack, and re-establish it at Roches Point in Georgina. In 1882, the government purchased 200 acres from James Roche and began laying out a new town with streets named after British army officers and lots reserved for an ambitious array of public buildings. That was as far as the scheme progressed, however, as Maitland was unable to convince the Crown of the merits of his vision.

Industry began to develop in earnest after railway lines encircled the lakeshores, exploiting the region's vast resources of lumber, fish, farm produce, limestone, and ice for refrigeration. These industries brought new wealth to the area and fuelled further growth, leading one-time sleepy villages to develop into towns bustling with energy. Though these industries are long gone today, the towns developed into modern cities—Barrie, Keswick, and Bradford—that remain at the heart of the region today.

Towards the end of the nineteenth century, vacationers started to come every summer, and cottages and resorts began to dot the lake's picturesque shoreline. Steamers took tourists around the lake, people headed out onto the waters in skiffs and canoes, and moonlight excursions became a particularly popular activity. Lake Simcoe became a place of leisure, and it largely remains so to this day. Lake Simcoe offers visitors a variety of attractions: resorts to unwind in, historical sites to explore, quaint communities, boat cruises on the lake, world-class angling (especially in winter—Lake Simcoe is widely reputed to be the best location for ice fishing in North America), and endless opportunities to engage in water sports.

Secrets of Lake Simcoe is a collection of stories that together reveal the historical importance of southern Ontario's largest interior lake. We have selected tales that encapsulate key moments and important facets in the lake's history, revealing as many of its secrets as can be contained within a book of this size. These stories are the basis for the unique character of the region in general, and in particular for the character of the vibrant communities, large and small, which ring Lake Simcoe today. But for every story mentioned in this book, there are still others which must remain a secret...at least for now.

In most cases, it's possible to visit the sites where these events unfolded. Indeed, one can circumnavigate the lake and stop at all the locations in a couple of days. Once on the spot, the visitor experience varies greatly. In some places—like The Briars, Sibbald Point Provincial Park, and Rogers Reservoir—that are geared towards tourists, one is presented with a remarkable experience that is rewarding and insightful. Here, history literally comes alive. In other cases, the past has been erased under modern developments or claimed by nature and one must use a great deal of imagination to "see" the past, and then only in the mind's eye. In any event, to travel to the spots where history unfolded is to gain a new appreciation for Lake Simcoe and its varied communities.

Chapter 1
Fort Willow and the Nine Mile Portage

Ontario is rich in nineteenth-century fortresses. A legacy of British colonialism, these fortresses grew out of a very real fear of American invasion, a fear that was realized during the War of 1812. Fort York, Fort Henry, Fort Niagara, Fort Wellington, and Fort George are all popular tourist attractions today. Fort Willow, by contrast, sees relatively few visitors each year. Perhaps that is because this War of 1812–era fort fell into ruin and is only partially reconstructed. Perhaps it is because few people expect to find a fort in the woods near Lake Simcoe, far from the battlefields of the War of 1812.

It was the winter of 1813, the second winter of the War

Entrance to Fort Willow

of 1812, and British fortunes in Canada had reached their lowest ebb. Though the handful of British regulars posted in Canada, supported ably by the Canadian militia and their Indian allies, had managed to stem every American invasion, the Royal Navy had not performed nearly as well on the Great Lakes. Lakes Ontario and Erie were all but lost and British lines of communication had been severed. Unless a new supply route could be found, His Majesty's forces in the west would wither away and all of British North America west of Lake Huron would fall to the enemy.

Though little-known today, the tiny, isolated Fort Willow and the Nine Mile Portage, a primitive trail weaving through some of Ontario's densest forests, played a vital role in reversing the situation and preserving the territorial integrity of Canada during the war.

The Nine Mile Portage had long been used by natives and fur traders as part of a trade route linking Lake Ontario to Georgian Bay. Beginning at present-day Toronto the route travelled overland, paralleling the Humber River for a time before turning northwest toward Lake Simcoe. Travellers would transfer into canoes at a point along the Holland River called Indian Landing (about 2.5 kilometres north of modern-day Holland Landing), then traverse Lake Simcoe to the head of Kempenfelt Bay. There, the Nine Mile Portage led through the wilderness to Willow Creek, which fed into the Nottawasaga River and eventually into Lake Huron at Wasaga Beach.

Though natives and fur traders had already trekked the route for years, the first written record of the Nine Mile Portage appears in the 1799 *Gazetteer*, which simply states, "To the westward is a large deep bay, called Kempenfelt Bay, from the head of which is a short carrying-place to the River Nottawasaga." This brief entry belies the portage's importance as a highway of commerce, over which hundreds of pelts were carried annually.

But it was not until the War of 1812 that the Nine Mile Portage took on any strategic significance. In the summer of 1813, American Commodore Oliver Hazard Perry defeated a

Royal Navy squadron on Lake Erie, securing control of that vital body of water in the Great Lakes chain. This victory cut the British lines of communication to the isolated garrisons on Lake Huron, and with the majority of British resources tied up in the war against Napoleon it would take a long time to assemble the forces needed to retake control.

Desperately searching for an alternate means of supplying their garrisons in the west, the British seized upon the potential of the old fur trade route. Even though the route was less than ideal for military purposes—along narrow paths snaking through impenetrable wilderness, down rivers incapable of supporting large crafts, and through a dense swamp every bit as formidable as Florida's Everglades—it was the best available option.

To make the Nine Mile Portage more suitable for the transport of supplies, significant resources were devoted to improving it over the winter of 1813. The trail was widened and stumps were painstakingly removed to ease the passage of carts and cannons, and for the first time it took on the appearance of a functional road. So important was this endeavour that it took precedence over all other war-related industries for a time, including that of building warships. Some three hundred men were brought in from the naval base at Kingston to help construct the road to Willow Creek.

In addition to improving the trail, a fort was hacked out of the dark forests on an escarpment overlooking the end of the pathway at Willow Creek. Fort Willow was intended to defend the route from attack and act as a supply depot for forces operating in the north. A contemporary described the location as a "hellish and malarial place," yet the fort was quite sizable and housed a significant garrison. Wilfred Jury, the archeologist who was the first to seriously excavate the fort, described the construction efforts in his book, *The Nine Mile Portage*:

> *In the frosty atmosphere, the ring of the axe and the steady blows of the hammer must have vibrated continuously through the woods as the great pines and oaks crashed, and 29 bateaux were constructed in the cold damp fastness of the Minesing Swamp.*

Fort Willow consisted of several log houses, a barn, and two strong, defensive blockhouses, surrounded by a stout palisade measuring 55 by 76 metres (180 by 250 feet). Beyond that was a string of earthworks and trenches. The garrison numbered 250 men at its peak, including twenty Royal Navy shipwrights brought in to build bateaux (14-metre- or 45-foot-long rowboats) for service on the river and Lake Huron. The bulk of the fighting force was composed of men from the Royal Newfoundland Regiment—hardy soldiers well accustomed to frontier warfare—as well as a token detachment of artillery.

The Herculean efforts in building Fort Willow and improving the Nine Mile Portage were vital to supplying Fort Mackinac, an isolated stronghold on Lake Huron and the key to the west. Without relief, the fort may well have fallen and the outcome of the war been far different; at the very least, Canada beyond the shores of Georgian Bay would have been assimilated into the United States.

Despite their valued contribution to the successful war effort, Fort Willow and the Nine Mile Portage were only of value to the British while the conflict lasted. When the war ended and the peace agreement was signed in 1814, the British government rapidly abandoned the isolated fort and the primitive trail it served. Nevertheless, Fort Willow and the Nine Mile Portage continued to play an important role for a time. Settlers trickled along it on their way to points further west, and civilian commerce replaced military traffic. Local Historian Andrew Hunter, in his book *A History of Simcoe County*, points out that the Nine Mile Portage "was the only highway over which traders, settlers and Indians passed for many years, and was therefore vastly important in the life of the district at the time." Sir John Thompson, the famed explorer of Canada's Rocky Mountains, even passed through on the return leg of one of his western voyages of discovery.

Two linked events eventually spelled the demise of the portage: the decision to move the Royal Navy's Lake Huron establishment to Penetanguishene; and the completion in

1818 of the Penetanguishene Road (Highway 93) through the interior of Simcoe County, constructed to serve the new naval base. Within a few years the Nine Mile Portage was largely abandoned. But it had one last hurrah in store, thanks to explorer Sir John Franklin.

Born in 1786, Sir John Franklin had entered the Royal Navy at the age of fourteen and soon proved himself a natural explorer. He found his calling while serving under his cousin Matthew Flinders on a coastal survey of Australia between 1801 and 1803 and was later second-in-command of an Arctic hydrographic cruise in 1818. Franklin returned to the Arctic for his first independent command, a journey of exploration into Canada's north from 1818 to 1821, during which his party surveyed the western shores of Hudson Bay as far as the Arctic Ocean.

By this stage, the desire to find the legendary Northwest Passage to the Pacific Ocean had become something of an obsession for the ambitious sailor, and there could be no doubt that he would return to Canada's north. He did so in 1825, setting out from Toronto and using the Nine Mile Portage to transport his bateaux into Lake Huron.

Franklin entered Lake Simcoe in April 1825, only to find Kempenfelt Bay bound by ice. After a few days the ice had still not begun to break up, but Franklin decided to proceed anyway, breaking channels through the ice with axes to make his way to the head of the Nine Mile Portage. David

Soules, a local settler, helped Franklin move his boats and supplies over the portage in an expeditious fashion. Soules, who had been active in the War of 1812 building bateaux at Fort Willow, knew the route well. But it was not only Soules' knowledge of the terrain that Franklin desired—it was also his pair of sturdy oxen, the only draft animals for many miles around, without which pulling the heavy boats overland would have been all but impossible.

Sir John Franklin's second Arctic expedition proved even more successful than the first. He and his men surveyed 2,028 kilometres (1,260 miles) of the northwestern coastline of North America, from the Mackenzie River to Point Beechey in Alaska. In so doing, he proved the existence of the Northwest Passage, an achievement for which he was justly knighted. Franklin's success only fuelled his obsession, laying the groundwork for his demise. During an attempt to navigate the Northwest Passage in 1845, Sir John Franklin and his entire crew were lost.

By this time the Nine Mile Portage was no longer in use and the forest was reclaiming Fort Willow. Soon, both were almost completely forgotten, and it would be more than a century before they were rediscovered by Wilfred Jury, who brought their remarkable history to light.

Two hundred years later the fort is being reconstructed to its 1812 state, under the Fort Willow Improvement Program. Several signs and maps have been erected on-site detailing the history and importance of the fort and the painstaking efforts to rebuild it. A fresh palisade stretches around two-thirds of the site, and foundations for the original buildings have been laid out. One of the most impressive displays is a bateau used in the making of the A&E film *The Crossing*, about George Washington's epic crossing of the Delaware River during the Revolutionary War. Outside the palisade, anyone searching among the trees may be rewarded by stumbling upon the earthworks hurriedly dug to defend the fort during the War of 1812.

As visitors walk through the gates they can almost hear the sounds of musket fire and the deafening roar of cannons, the echoes of a destructive war long ago. It doesn't take much imagination to find yourself transported back to a time when the young nation of Canada was in peril from foreign invaders, a time when Fort Willow was a key to the country's survival.

Despite its importance in the war, few people know of Fort Willow, perhaps because of its out-of-the-way location. Only nine miles from the city of Barrie, the fort nonetheless feels secluded, as if it is consciously hiding from the modern world. This only enhances its appeal as a historic site.

Chapter 2
William Rains and His Colony

The township of Georgina is located on the southeastern shore of Lake Simcoe. While many of its early settlers fit the mould of hardy, hard-working pioneers, William Kingdom Rains was about as far from that idealized image as a man could be.

Rains was born in Wales in 1789 to a wealthy family with strong military roots. Educated in some of the finest schools in Britain, by the time he was a teenager he was well versed in literature, science, mathematics, and politics, and spoke at least four foreign languages—French, Italian, Greek, and Latin. Rains also studied ballroom dancing, art, and the piano.

William Rains and His Colony

The French Revolution, which eventually led to the rise of Napoleon Bonaparte as Emperor of France and propelled Europe into almost three decades of conflict, broke out a year after Rains' birth. Wars would play a significant part in his life. When he was sixteen, his father purchased for him a lieutenancy in the Royal Regiment of Artillery. While Rains was a true student of the art of war and a dedicated officer, he was also known as something of a dandy. An incurable carouser and womanizer, who has been described as "a jovial gentleman, notorious for his success with the fairer sex," he was considered the best-dressed man in his regiment and was not above personalizing his regular-issue dress in the name of fashion. He also moved in high circles and frequented lavish parties. One of his closest friends was reputed to be the noted author Lord Byron.

Rains saw extensive service in Portugal and Spain under the Duke of Wellington between 1807 and 1813, rising to the rank of Captain. He was eventually made a Knight of the Imperial Order of St. Leopold by Francis I of Austria, in recognition of a brilliant military career.

Despite his habitual womanizing, the young gentleman was expected to eventually take a wife, and so, on August 15, 1811, Major Rains finally wed. He did so quite reluctantly, however, his journal entry for his wedding day reading, "married and be damned with it." Marriage vows or not, Rains did not give up his sexual adventures and continued to enjoy the company of his mistresses.

After the war, he was retired on half pay and settled on his family's estate, Sutton Lodge, in Wales. A short while later, however, he moved to England to practice engineering. In 1824 he re-enlisted in the army. Some suggest that he missed the excitement of military life, though it's equally likely that he was attempting to distance himself from a marriage that, despite producing eleven children, was loveless and tense.

Rains remained in the army only a few short years before emigrating to Canada, settling along the shores of Lake Simcoe. True to form, he didn't bring his wife with him. Instead, he found warmth on cold winter nights in the arms of a pair of beautiful young sisters—sixteen-year-old Frances Doubleday and her younger sister Eliza—whom he had met on the transatlantic voyage. Newly orphaned, they had no place to stay in Canada and nobody to support them. Rains had known their father and offered to share his home with them. Frances and Eliza were swept away by the dashing officer and readily agreed. In time, a complicated but apparently contented love triangle developed, with Rains taking both sisters as his wives. Strange as it may seem, the three were blissfully happy together, and numerous children resulted from the double marriage.

Like many retired officers, Rains chose to settle in Georgina, building a rough cabin named Penn Rains, overlooking Lake Simcoe. But although he owned prime real estate along Lake Simcoe's shores, Rains wasn't entirely satisfied. Ever since seeing a surveyor's map of Upper Canada (as Ontario was then known) while posted in Malta, Rains had dreamed of establishing a colony somewhere in Canada. His mind returned to such endeavours shortly after he settled in Georgina.

In 1834 Rains pitched a proposal to the government of Upper Canada in which he asked to be granted St. Joseph Island in Lake Huron as the site for his new colony. He planned to settle one hundred families on this remote island, located near the point where Lakes Huron, Superior, and Michigan all merge. Sir John Colborne, then the Lieutenant-Governor of Canada, was supportive of the scheme but could not give the land freely. Instead, Rains was forced to purchase the land, a total of five thousand acres, at a cost of one shilling per acre.

Over the winter of 1834–35 Rains gathered investors to fund the colony. More than half a dozen men stepped forward, and in the spring of 1835 Rains, his two wives, and several other families sailed aboard the Georgian Bay steamer *Penetanguishene* for their new home. Rains said goodbye to his Georgina lands, which he sold to Susan Sibbald, and which today form the heart of Sibbald Point Provincial Park.

On St. Joseph Island the settlers built a sawmill and log homes, cleared trees for farm fields, and settled in with their families. Over the next few years the *Penetanguishene* brought other families, and shipped out enough lumber to make the colony mildly profitable. Rains basked in the glory. He had founded his own settlement, which seemed to have a bright future, and he was made the island's Magistrate and Justice of the Peace. Like the aristocratic landholders of old, Rains held almost total power in the little colony.

The success did not last, however. Investors, disappointed by the meagre profits, began to back out. The sawmill soon closed, and the steamer stopped supplying the island on a regular basis. As conditions began to deteriorate on St. Joseph Island, people slowly began to leave. By 1839 only eight families remained on the island, and the number dwindled further, so that by the mid 1840s none remained except Rains and his family. Having lost his fortune in the failed scheme, and with nowhere else to go, he stayed on at St. Joseph even as the forest consumed the abandoned buildings.

In June 1848, the famous biologist Louis Agassiz and his research team, en route to Lake Superior, found their canoes threatened by a rapidly approaching storm. The men headed for the safety of St. Joseph Island, where they hastily erected a camp in which to wait out the rain and wind. Imagine their surprise when a dishevelled man, looking something like Robinson Crusoe, emerged from the forest and greeted the travellers with the sophisticated manners of an English gentleman. The strange hermit invited Agassiz back to his house for the night, and he cautiously agreed.

Agassiz was led to a log cabin, a humble home that

was rough in appearance, like its owner. Inside, however, the home was filled from floor to ceiling with books on every subject, many written in French, Italian, and Greek. Over dinner and throughout the evening, Rains spoke poetically and passionately about politics, science, and literature. Agassiz was confused. His host was clearly cultured, but here he was living on a bush farm far from civilization. Intrigued, he asked the man his name, and the stranger introduced himself as Major William Kingdom Rains.

Despite the loneliness and primitive conditions on the island, it seems that Rains and his women were perfectly content. In fact, they had as many as twenty-three children between them, many of whom became well known in the region and respected for their various endeavours. Rains, seemingly unconcerned that the colony he had hoped to establish had failed miserably, died on the island, as did his "wives."

Although William Rains was flighty, vain, and had questionable morals, he did leave one important legacy behind him. The town of Sutton, originally called Bourchier's Mills, was renamed when community founder James O'Brien Bourchier lost a poker game to Rains. The prize was the chance to rename the town. Rains chose Sutton, after his family estate in England.

Chapter 3
William Sibbald,
A Reluctant Groom

William Sibbald was a reluctant groom who had to be encouraged with liquor to even take his marriage vows. But despite his misgivings, he soon found himself in love with the woman who was forced upon him. It was a powerful love that grew stronger over time.

The tragic story of love and loss really begins with William's mother, Susan Sibbald. Susan was a wealthy lady who owned several ancestral estates in her native country, Britain. She had nine sons, two of whom—William and Charles—had emigrated to Upper Canada (Ontario) in the early 1830s. Like any mother, Susan worried about her children and even after they grew into adulthood she still felt responsible for their well-being. So when, in 1835, the fifty-two year old mother heard rumours that William and Charles were struggling in their new country, were forced to reside in a tavern, and were perhaps slipping under the influence of the demon drink, she immediately booked a passage to Canada to save them.

After a lengthy and gruelling voyage, and numerous hardships for a lady travelling on her own, Mrs. Sibbald found her sons and was relieved to see that they were living well and comfortably in Orillia, and doing much better then she had been led to believe. But, intent on keeping a watchful eye on her sons, she elected to settle on an estate at what is

Eldon Hall, circa 1900

now Sibbald Point in Georgina and sent for the remainder of her family to join her there. Her home, Eildon Hall, is today the centerpiece of Sibbald Point Provincial Park.

Once settled and with her family by her side, Susan Sibbald learned that one of her neighbours was Captain Simon Lee, an extremely wealthy man and a former employee of the British East India Company, the largest mercantile business in the world at the time. The company was so large that it actually governed India and maintained a private army. Captain Lee had unwed daughters and Susan Sibbald had several bachelor sons, so there was hope that a union would occur between the two aristocratic families. Lee considered William Sibbald a perfect candidate for his firstborn, Emily Buxton. William was handsome, bright, wealthy, and well educated, and had a charm that young women could not resist. He would make a fine husband for any eligible lady.

There was one glaring problem with this plan—William hardly seemed to notice Emily. Instead, he only had eyes for her vivacious younger sister, Mary Ready. William desperately wanted to court Mary Ready, but the tradition of the time insisted that daughters marry in order of age. Emily Buxton, being the eldest, should be wed first. William meant no disrespect, but he could not resist his feelings for Mary. She was beautiful, while her sister was rather plain, in his eyes. And unlike her reserved and proper older sibling, Mary Ready was outgoing and fun-loving. She was not bound to the conventional ways that a woman should behave, which William found exhilarating and a breath of fresh air compared to other girls he had known. He was smitten, and had his heart set on marriage.

William had no intention of carrying on a relationship with Mary Ready behind her father's back, so he approached Captain Lee for permission to court her. He did so with all the naïve optimism of a young man in love, but his hopes were soon crushed. Captain Lee and his wife insisted that their daughters marry in order of age. Therefore, if young Sibbald intended to ask for the hand of one of their daughters, that hand had to be Emily's. William was shocked and deeply saddened. He couldn't bring himself to marry Emily when he was so deeply in love with Mary Ready. How could he promise to love and cherish Emily when his heart was already given to another woman? William simply wouldn't do it. Unfortunately, Captain Lee was equally stubborn and refused to budge on the matter. William could not have and would *never* have his permission to wed Mary Ready.

Broken-hearted, William decided that if he could not have the woman he wanted he would simply not get married. But his mother had other plans for him. Susan urged William to reconsider. After all, he needed a wife, whether in his grief he thought so or not, and while Emily may not have captured his heart in the same way as Mary Ready, Susan assured him he would grow to love her as the years went on. Susan saw in

Emily attributes that were invisible to her son.

At first William resisted his mother's constant pressure to marry Emily and start a family of his own. He was set in his ways and could not let go of Mary Ready. But eventually he began to accept that he could never have the woman he desperately wanted and that he would need to move on with his life. He then realized that his mother was right and that Emily would make a devoted and hard-working wife. Finally, reluctantly, William accepted Captain Lee's proposal and agreed to make Emily his bride.

But on the day of the wedding William began to get cold feet. He kept thinking of Mary Ready's sweet smile, the smile he had fallen in love with. But now he was going to marry her sister. It seemed like a cruel joke. William was so reluctant to follow through with the ceremony that he needed the encouragement of liberal doses of brandy to even go to the altar and then needed to be forcibly restrained from fleeing. It was hardly a romantic beginning to William and Emily's lives together.

Time passed and William slowly began to see something in his new wife that had been masked behind the walls imposed by proper conduct for young women. He discovered in Emily an inner beauty that he never noticed before and realized she was everything a man could want or hope for in a wife. Eventually the pair fell deeply in love with one another, and despite the rocky beginning, their marriage was a happy one. Not only did they share a deep passion, but they also became each other's best friend. They were inseparable, together facing head-on whatever life could throw their way.

Sadly, their time together was far too short. Emily died on April 8, 1854 at the tender age of twenty-eight. Something died that day within William too. The light in his heart was extinguished forever. As he grieved at the bedside of his wife, William must surely have reflected on the cruelty of fate: here was a woman he had originally not wanted to marry at all, but whose kindness and warmth had caused him to fall so deeply in love that her loss was overwhelming. The trauma left him scarred, a changed man.

It is no surprise that William never remarried: William and Emily had developed a deep emotional bond that grew with every year they spent together, facing life's challenges and enjoying its simple pleasures. It was a bond so strong it could not be broken, and William carried Emily's memory in his heart for the remainder of his days. The once reluctant groom had found true love in spite of his initial misgivings.

Chapter 4
The Ghost Canal

While the Lake Simcoe region has nothing to compare to such marvels as the pyramids of Egypt, the castles of Europe, or the skyscrapers of New York, it nonetheless has seen impressive architectural and engineering feats.

By any standards, the Trent-Severn Waterway is an engineering masterpiece, and is justifiably well known. The waterway is an expansive system of locks and lakes linking Lake Ontario with Lake Huron—of which Lake Simcoe is a vital component. But little is ever heard of an ill-fated canal which, had it been completed, might have become equally famous.

Overgrown with creeping vines and partially filled with swaying grasses, weathered concrete ruins lurk forebodingly in a corner of East Gwillimbury. Few people know of these

The Ghost Canal

forgotten vestiges of the past, and those who do refer to them as the "Ghost Canal." On a stormy night, with talons of lightning clawing from the sky, the grim stone ruins would certainly appear frightful, but there's nothing supernatural about the canal. It does, however, represent a haunting reminder of one man's obsession to link Newmarket to Lake Simcoe by water.

The remnants of the Ghost Canal are surrounded by

tranquil woods and wild fields. Here, far removed from modernity, it is easy to imagine you are in the year 1909, when work was proceeding at a feverish pace and excitement over the project was high. People looked forward to the day when they would watch as passenger boats lined with tourists and heavily loaded barges slowly sailed by. But the canal was never completed, and if you look down into the massive lock today you see swaying grass where water should be. Despite being one of Ontario's greatest engineering follies, the Ghost Canal captures the imagination with an intoxicating mixture of mystery and history.

The story of these little-known ruins begins in 1904, when William Mulock, then Minister of Labour and Public Works in the Liberal government of Sir Wilfred Laurier, began pressing for a canal to link his native Newmarket with the Trent-Severn Waterway system running from Lake Ontario to Georgian Bay. The proposed canal would follow the Holland River from Cook's Bay on Lake Simcoe to Newmarket, or perhaps even Aurora, and was intended to boost local industry and tourism.

Although Mulock took the credit, the idea of a canal linking Newmarket to Lake Simcoe had existed for many years. In fact, as early as 1820 there had been ambitious plans to construct a canal linking Lake Ontario to Lake Simcoe along the Rouge and Holland river systems. For most of the nineteenth century such projects remained no more than dreams, but in 1851 an entrepreneur named Rowland Burr decided to make the plan a reality. It was Burr's dream to build a canal linking Lake Ontario to Lake Huron, providing a shorter route for steamships laden with cargo. The canal was a project that, if it were successful, would guarantee his place among the greatest builders in Ontario's history. In fact, if the canal had been completed, it would likely have *shaped* Ontario's history.

Rowland Burr was born in 1798 in Buck's County, Pennsylvania, the second son of Quaker carpenter Reuben Burr. By 1810 the family had immigrated to Ontario and settled in Aurora. Rowland apprenticed under his father and by the age of seventeen was considered a master builder in his own right. He was ready to set out on his own and travelled widely in search of opportunities. He would scout out a location in southern York Region, where rivers ran strong and consistent, and there build a sawmill, gristmill, or woollen mill. He also built homes nearby for the workers that the mills would attract. Then he would sell the lot for a handsome profit and move on to repeat the process elsewhere. In so doing, Burr founded several communities, including Headford and Woodbridge (originally called Burwick in his honour).

By the 1850s, Burr was worth $70,000. In today's currency he would be a millionaire many times over. But he wanted to leave his mark, and that's where the proposed Lake

Ontario and Georgian Bay Canal came in. The idea seemed sound enough on paper. Water transportation was generally cheaper for industry than rail, because products could be shipped in larger quantities. In addition, the proposed canal would present a shorter route from the west to the St. Lawrence River than the Lake Huron–Lake Erie–Lake Ontario route then in use.

Buoyed by this rationale, Burr personally surveyed several possible routes on foot. The one he settled upon would run up the Humber River from its mouth in Lake Ontario and then down the Holland River to Lake Simcoe. From there, the canal would join the Severn River and run out to Lake Huron via Georgian Bay. Because it would pass through Newmarket, it was no surprise that local businessmen and politicians rushed to support Burr's proposal. The Lake Ontario and Georgian Bay Canal, as it was called, would provide a cheap outlet for local produce, entice new industry to town, and perhaps offer a source of income from service-based businesses such as hotels and taverns.

The people of Newmarket were not the only ones who were excited by the canal, however. Many Great Lakes port communities, Chicago among them, were enthused by the idea. Any means of delivering wheat to the eastern cities cheaply and efficiently was looked upon with interest by Midwestern businessmen.

The project gathered momentum in 1857, when

The Ghost Canal

Parliament passed an act authorizing the Lake Ontario and Georgian Bay Canal. Surveys were commissioned, and there was even a sod-turning ceremony in 1859. That is when Burr's scheme started to collapse. It was soon determined that the Humber and Holland Rivers were too shallow for the large vessels that were intended to use the canal, and that the Oak Ridge Moraine's sudden increase in elevation would require more locks than originally thought. With dredging and enough locks the canal could work, in theory, but the cost would be an astronomical $30 million.

To all intents and purposes the Lake Ontario and Georgian Bay canal was dead. Nevertheless, Rowland Burr continued to campaign for its construction and maintained his belief in its potential until his death in 1865.

Plans for the canal lay dormant for almost half a century until William Mulock revived them in 1904. His vision was more modest than Burr's, intending to take the canal only as far as Newmarket, or perhaps Aurora. But politics, far more than practicality, dictated the development of the Newmarket Canal. In fact, from the start, it was wrought with political favouritism. In addition to being Minister of Labour and Public Works, William Mulock was Newmarket's elected Member of Parliament. He had lured many industries to the community, and therefore knew his political career depended upon the prosperity of Newmarket's economy. In the face of rising railway freight fees that threatened the survival of these businesses, Mulock revived the canal scheme. Water shipping, it was thought, would be a cheaper alternative to rail.

Mulock originally presented the idea to the local business community on September 4, 1904, and helped organize a delegation to Ottawa during February of the following year. He also organized a lobby in Parliament to support the project and ensure that the petition for the canal was warmly received. Because of his efforts, which were motivated principally to save his own career, the project was given the green light, despite mounting evidence that it would face daunting engineering obstacles.

Events were to become even more interesting. The Railways and Canals Department, which fell under Mulock's Ministry, was vehemently opposed to the concept of the Newmarket Canal. The bureaucrats preferred railroads as a mode of transportation, and saw Mulock's plan as running counter to their own efforts and interests. In a remarkable example of governmental backstabbing, they altered the dimensions of the canal to make it prohibitively expensive to build, a move that they anticipated would sour legislators on the concept.

They were wrong. The project went ahead anyway.

When word reached Newmarket that the canal was to become reality, people were joyous. This was the most exciting prospect for the community in generations, and once again everyone was sure it would lead to unprecedented prosperity. Residents looked to the future with a sense of optimism. As for Mulock, he rode a wave of popularity to an easy re-election in 1905. His plan had worked to perfection. Now all that remained was for the canal to be built.

Construction of the canal was an engineering nightmare. Extensive dredging of the shallow Holland River was required, as was the construction of storage tanks to collect whatever water could be gathered from spring floods, and the installation of several locks and dams. In addition, retaining walls, pipe culverts, swing bridges, and docks would all have to be built. It was a massive and complex undertaking.

Work was undertaken in two stages and was expected to take as long as a decade to complete. The first section, from Lake Simcoe to Holland Landing, a distance of 14.5 kilometres (9 miles), was at lake level and therefore required no lock structures. The second section, from Holland Landing to Newmarket, would require three locks over a distance of 6.5 kilometres (4 miles) to cover the 14-metre (45-foot) rise in elevation. A proposed third section would carry the canal as far as Aurora, but this was held off for the future.

Within a few years, many people began to have second thoughts about the canal. It seemed like an awfully large and expensive enterprise for the few passenger steamers or freight barges that could be expected to use it each season.

And would it even work? With the best engineering minds on the project there were still serious doubts that the Holland River could accommodate ships with anything but the shallowest of drafts. Still, the naysayers were silenced by the powerful voices of Laurier and Mulock, and work continued. By 1911 about two-thirds of the canal was complete, including three lift-locks, three swing bridges, and a turning basin, at the then-astronomical cost of $600,000.

The year 1911 was pivotal. National elections saw Sir Wilfred Laurier's Liberal government pitted against Robert Borden's Conservatives, who were buoyed by widespread anger over the government's propensity for wasteful spending on ambitious but ill-conceived projects. To no one's surprise, Borden won the election. Even the people of Newmarket, who had the most to gain by the canal, voted decisively against Laurier. With the change of government, construction on the Newmarket Canal was halted and ultimately abandoned. In subsequent years, the canal began to be derisively known as "Mulock's Folly" or "Mulock's Madness," casting a dark shadow over an otherwise illustrious career.

It is ironic that a project which had helped sweep a Laurier stalwart back into office in 1905 was partly responsible for the downfall of the same government six years later. Perhaps it was fitting for a scheme that was always motivated more by politics than practicality.

Today, the turning basin where boats would have swung

around for a return trip up the canal has been filled in to become a parking lot, much of the canal has become overgrown, and several of the swing bridges are long gone. However, some remains of what has eerily been called the "Ghost Canal" remain. One lock structure may be seen in the village of Holland Landing where old Yonge Street enters the village. Another, the most picturesque and the best to visit, lies amidst the meadows and wetlands of Rogers Reservoir, accessed off Green Lane. Here, visitors can see the 8-metre-deep lock in all its majesty and gain an appreciation for the scale of the project. They can also follow a trail that parallels the route of the canal to Green Lane, where the last remaining swing bridge stands forgotten and neglected.

These ruins are all that remains of William Mulock's dashed dreams for a canal linking Newmarket to Lake Simcoe. Like an apparition, the project would remain incomplete and would haunt the great politician for the remainder of his days. It was indeed the greatest folly of his career, but the Ghost Canal is now one of the area's most evocative ruins and a reminder of a fascinating era in Lake Simcoe's history.

Chapter 5
The Loss of
the *Morning*

A fresh, frosty breeze swept over the deck and found the back of the captain's neck. All around, crowds of passengers milled about, chatting amiably and admiring the beautiful fall weather. None seemed concerned by the clouds gathering in the distance or the white tips forming on the waves. But the captain was. He made mental calculations and decided that if a storm was indeed brewing, his little steamer may not reach the safety of port before it hit. Turning up the collar of his overcoat, the captain cast a loving gaze over the elegant vessel, his eyes finally resting on the board atop the pilot-house which proudly displayed the vessel's name—*Morning*.

The Loss of the Morning

Before the coming of rail and road networks, water provided the quickest, most comfortable, and most efficient means of transportation in Ontario. As a result, for the better part of the nineteenth century Lake Simcoe played a major part in the development of central Ontario. Settlers opening up the interior passed over her waters, and all manner of goods were shipped across her expanse. Originally, the boats plying the lake were canoes paddled by natives and fur traders, bateaux, and even a few sailing vessels. By the 1830s, such vessels were being replaced by steamships.

Throughout the nineteenth century a vast number of industries relied on Lake Simcoe to ship their products. Farmers, quarriers, fur traders, millers, and especially logging companies transported their goods by steamship to one of the handful of lakeside communities that were linked to railway lines. From this point, the produce, stone, furs, flour, and lumber would be shipped to distant markets in Toronto, and even the United States. On their return the ships brought mail, freight, settlers, and guests for lakeside resorts. A reliable transportation network was vital for economic development and stability, and Lake Simcoe provided that.

The sight of smoke billowing from a ship's stack was a common one around the lake for close to a century, as a small fleet of steamships dominated the lake's waters. Among the steamers that criss-crossed the lake were well-known vessels like the *Morning*, the *Enterprise*, and the *Otonabee*. Eventually, when a network of rail lines had been laid across Central Ontario, and later with the onset of the automobile era, these steamships found themselves obsolete and out of work. Most were simply abandoned, either scuttled in the water or beached along the shores and allowed to rot. Others had more dramatic endings, either going up in flames or sinking to a watery grave.

The *Morning* was one of the earliest steamships to ply the waters of Lakes Simcoe and Couchiching in the nineteenth century. She was the brainchild and proud possession of Charles Poulett Thompson, a man better known for his interests in stagecoaches than steamships.

As early as 1833, Thompson was operating a line of daily stagecoaches along Yonge Street, running from Toronto in the south to Lake Simcoe in the north. Augmenting his service was the steamer *Sir John Colborne*, on which passengers, mail, and cargo were transported across Lake Simcoe. It was the first steamer to appear on Lake Simcoe, but the *Sir John Colborne* was less than successful—a slow vessel with an annoying habit of getting stuck in the mud of Cook's Bay. Later, Thompson added stage lines in Simcoe County, particularly along the Penetanguishene Road that ran from Barrie to Georgian Bay. In so doing, he created a seamless transportation line that ran from Lake Ontario to Lake Huron through the heart of central Ontario. Thompson ruled the transportation business along this route for more than a quarter of a century.

To complete his monopoly over transportation in central Ontario, in 1844 Thompson joined forces with Lake Simcoe shipping mogul William Laughton. It seemed their business interests perfectly complemented one another, and for a while the partnership was successful and harmonious. Together they built the modern sidewheel steamship *Beaver* at Point Mara, a vessel that replaced the aging *Sir John Colborne* and served to strengthen their hold over the movement of people and goods on Lake Simcoe. Despite their success in business, the partnership between the two men was not an easy one. Both were ambitious, perhaps arrogant individuals, who entered into the relationship with an eye toward its benefits to their own business interests.

By the late 1840s, only five years after they had pooled their resources, Thompson and Laughton began to have differences of opinion on personal and professional matters. The arguments grew so heated and so frequent that in 1849 the partnership was dissolved, with Laughton remaining as sole owner of the *Beaver*. The end of the relationship was unpleasant, and much bad blood remained between the two men.

The animosity only grew more heated when Thompson built his own steamship, the *Morning*, to rival Laughton's for control of Lakes Simcoe and Couchiching. The *Morning* was a fine and attractive sidewheeler, measuring about 40 metres (130 feet) in the keel, with lounges for passengers below deck and a sheltered pilothouse aft. Her most distinctive feature, however, was an unusually tall smokestack. More importantly from a commercial point of view, she was several knots faster than Laughton's vessel. As a result, Thompson began to steal business away from his erstwhile partner, and to threaten his company's survival.

Enraged, Laughton responded by adding his own stage line, called the People's Line of Stages, operating along Yonge Street. The former partners had become fierce rivals and were willing to go to great lengths to undermine their competitor. The war between the two was no-holds-barred and particularly bitter, but the decisive battles were always fought between the opposing steamships on Lake Simcoe.

The *Morning* travelled to all the ports along Lake Simcoe, as well as Orillia on Lake Couchiching, stopping in each community at least twice per week. The *Beaver* did pretty much the same. Unfortunately, at this time there was simply not enough business for both. One would have to go. The competition to see which would prevail was cutthroat and, at times, almost laughable. Both owners introduced lower and lower rates in an effort to secure Lake Simcoe's traffic, and to introduce more and more frills. Soon, meals and bands were included free of charge, and tickets cost a mere pittance. It was a farce, and it couldn't last forever.

The Loss of the Morning

After a few years of this one-upmanship, it was Laughton who bowed out and retired to Bell Ewart, leaving Thompson sole dominion over Lakes Simcoe and Couchiching and as the undisputed king of the Yonge Street–Lake Simcoe transportation route. He was at his peak, and it was said with only slight exaggeration that he "owned a share in every stage that was running in Ontario." He was also lord over all shipping on Lake Simcoe, earning him the nickname "Steamboat" Thompson.

But "Steamboat" Thompson did not have long to celebrate the victory over his one-time partner. By 1853 the Northern Railway extended all the way up Yonge Street to Barrie, making Thompson's stagecoaches obsolete. Thompson, nearly bankrupt, was forced to sell his steamship. The Northern Railway purchased the *Morning* and began to operate her in tandem with their trains, shipping passengers and goods from the station in Barrie to communities all over the lakes. She continued to ply the waters for nearly a decade, spending most of that time as the sole steamer on Lakes Simcoe and Couchiching.

And she likely would have continued in her role for several more years, if not for a sudden autumn squall in 1862. A chill breeze whipping across the lake soon turned into a howling wind, with a fierce thunderstorm nipping at its heels. The captain's fears of being trapped out on the lake in the midst of an autumn storm were realized. He watched helplessly as he wind gained velocity with each passing minute and the waves were transformed into heaving mountains that pounded the little steamship. The captain turned her towards Roches Point, desperate to reach safe harbour, but the *Morning* was at the mercy of the lake and was tossed around like a toy. Her unfortunate passengers and crew could only stare into the face of death as they waited in terror for the ship to take her final plunge into the lake's depths.

Yet the captain's calm never wavered. Using every ounce of his skill and experience he managed to keep the vessel afloat. Passengers and crew swore he kept the ship from sinking by sheer stubbornness alone. But despite expert seamanship the *Morning* was swept onto a shoal off Roches Point and grounded there. Thankfully, once the storm subsided everyone aboard was safely rescued, but the storm presaged an early onslaught of winter and there was no time to free the steamer before the lake froze over.

That winter, ice freed the sidewheeler from the shoal, and spring found her deposited in the shallows near Roches Point. Unfortunately, her hull had been severely damaged by the violent grounding in the fall and the pressure of the ice all winter, so the Northern Railway declined to salvage her. The *Morning* was left to rot where she lay, and within a matter of years she had been swallowed by the lake.

As for Charles Poulett Thompson, after selling the *Morning* he shifted his business focus to the thriving town of Barrie, where he became a prominent citizen and had a hand in the construction of several landmark buildings. The contracts for Simcoe County's first courthouse and jail, the latter still standing, was awarded to him. But he never again rose to his earlier dizzying heights when, with the aid of the steamship *Morning,* he had a monopoly on transportation in the Lake Simcoe region.

Chapter 6
The *Matilda* Mystery

Despite its natural beauty and the calming influence of its blue waters, Lake Simcoe and its environs have seen their share of violent acts. In fact, the course of the lake's history can be traced in blood. While we can assume the native population saw its share of killing—the murder of fur trader Etienne Brûlé and the wholesale slaughter of Jesuit missionaries and their Huron allies in Huronia suggest as much—the first murder on record occurred shortly after European settlers arrived. The Lake Simcoe area was still wilderness when, in 1824, Corporal James Cannon, who watched over government stores at Fort Willow and operated a tavern, was killed for his rumoured hoard of wealth.

Since then, many other lives have been claimed by

The Matilda *Mystery*

A sailing sloop like the Matilda

human hands, leaving a shameful legacy for the region. Two murders in particular seem to have entered local lore. One was the apparent quadruple-murder aboard the sailboat *Matilda*. We will explore the other in the next chapter.

In October of 1866, the sailing sloop *Matilda* disappeared beneath the waters of Cook's Bay, taking four young lives with her. The only survivor was a good-for-nothing named George Doolittle. Doolittle's varying accounts of the fateful voyage were conflicting in their details, and in many cases so full of lies and obvious misdirection that they carried little weight. It was clear to investigators that he was hiding something, but what? Was it multiple murders, as many came to suspect? The true story of what happened aboard that vessel remains one of Lake Simcoe's most enduring mysteries.

The *Matilda* was owned by Captain McCullough of Orillia, and was one of numerous vessels plying the waters of Lakes Simcoe and Couchiching transporting goods from one port to another. In the summer of 1866, the *Matilda* had collided with the steamship *Emily May* in the Narrows connecting the two lakes. The *Emily May* escaped lightly, but the impact caused structural damage to the *Matilda*. Taking on water through her hull, the sloop limped into Orillia and spent the remainder of the season moored alongside the wharf, awaiting repair.

On Saturday, October 13, while Captain McCullough was away, the devious George Doolittle approached Mrs. McCullough and inquired about borrowing the ship. He lied to her, vowing that her husband had already given him permission. Doolittle had a poor reputation around town as a drunkard and a "shiftless kind of fellow, never caring to work if he could by any means avoid it." Mrs. McCullough flatly refused his request. Whether his unsavory reputation played a part in her decision is unknown, but she could not in good conscience allow anyone to sail out into the storm-tossed autumn waters of Lake Simcoe in a vessel that was not seaworthy.

Doolittle was undeterred. Under the cover of darkness he quietly slipped aboard the *Matilda*. He was accompanied by his wife, two daughters, and a young lad named Alex (or Adam) Birch, a native of Barrie. Silently, they cast off and headed out into the moonlit waters, heading for the town of Sutton. According to Doolittle's later testimony, a sudden storm came howling across Lake Simcoe and began tossing the *Matilda* around. Buffeted by wild wind and crashing water, the tears in the ship's hull ripped open further. Where previously only a trickle of water was pooling in her hold, now there was a torrent.

Doolittle realized that the ship was beginning to sink and alerted his wife to the danger. She handed him one of their children, then raced below deck for the other, who was still sound asleep in her bunk (this despite the pandemonium topside—one of many odd statements in Doolittle's account). While his wife was below, the gybing mainsail supposedly swung across and blindsided Doolittle, knocking the child out of his hands and into the angry waters. Instantly, the baby was swallowed up by the waters and lost. Doolittle, according to his testimony, was powerless to save the child. By this point, the *Matilda* was sinking so fast that Doolittle barely made it to the ship's small lifeboat. His wife never emerged from below deck. As the ship slipped beneath the waves she and her second child were trapped by the inrushing water. The ship's hold became their tomb.

As for Alex Birch, Doolittle never could decide upon his fate. In one account, the last he saw of the young man was as he jumped from the swamped bow into the turbulent water. In another, he was in the skiff and then presumably washed overboard by a massive wave that crashed over the boat. And in yet another version he was last seen walking aft on the ship. In any event, Birch was claimed by the lake that night as well. Doolittle was the only survivor.

Alone in a small rowboat, Doolitle made for the nearest point of land, which happened to be Fox Island, off Georgina. He was discovered a few days later, cold and hungry, but otherwise none the worse for wear. Immediately after his rescue newspapers began following the story, and the more that reporters dug the more a foul stench began to emerge. The *Barrie Northern Advance*, for example, noted "the circumstances [of the incident] look rather gloomy and suspicious." Almost everyone who took note of the tragedy—reporters, police investigators, readers who eagerly followed the story in local papers—believed that Doolittle had killed the other passengers. It was the only way to explain the wildly different versions of the events, and his suspicious behaviour that night and in the days that followed. And yet, no charges were ever laid. There was simply no concrete evidence against the man.

What happened aboard the *Matilda* that night remains a tragic mystery. Were four people murdered? Did a desperate man alter his story to cover up his own negligence and cowardice? Only one man knew the true story, and he went to his grave unwilling to share it.

In the 140 years since the event, some have questioned

whether the victims themselves might be trying to reveal the nature of their demise. How else does one explain the sightings of a mist-shrouded sailing vessel plying Cook's Bay with ghostly passengers lined up on deck? These sightings, few in number but chilling in nature, might easily be dismissed as the result of one too many beers, too much sun, or perhaps even outright fabrication. But could it be that the dead are pointing otherworldly fingers at a murderer gone free?

It is unlikely that anyone will ever discover the truth of what happened out on the waters of Lake Simcoe that autumn night in 1866. As the years pass, fact and fiction become hopelessly blended together into folklore. It is said that the water keeps her secrets, and it certainly seems so in this case. The events aboard the doomed *Matilda* are destined to remain an unsolved mystery.

Chapter 7
The Sinking of the *Enterprise*

*Her bows were up, and the great square
doors in them, through which her hawsers
came out, made her look like a big dead
fish. Her stern was well under. There was no
doubt about it. She had sunk!*

Such was the scene at the Barrie wharf in 1903 as seen through the eyes of Arthur Lower, a famed historian who witnessed the sinking of the steamship *Enterprise* as a child and later wrote of it in the *Queen's Quarterly*. The sight of the *Enterprise* wallowing in the shallows like a beached whale, and just as helpless, was one that few ever forgot. But it should not have been a surprise. The *Enterprise* was never considered among the better steamships plying the waters of lakes Simcoe and Couchiching. She was ungainly and unattractive, and by the last years of her forty-year career she was downright unseaworthy. The people of lakeshore communities from Beaverton in the east to Barrie in the west nonetheless had a warm place in their hearts for her.

The *Enterprise* had a less than glorious origin. Built in 1868 by James McPherson, she was originally a simple transport schooner called the *Couchiching*. McPherson was a prosperous farmer, successful politician—he was elected reeve fourteen times—and entrepreneur who operated a booming quarry in Rama. The ship was employed carrying lime from Quarry Point at Rama to ports all around lakes Simcoe and Couchiching. She served in this capacity for more than a decade, but it wasn't long before railways encircled the lakes and made the *Couchiching* obsolete. Lime could be transported faster and more efficiently by train than by ship.

With the vessel no longer needed in its original role, McPherson refitted her as a passenger boat in 1883. He cut down the mast, built several additional decks, installed a steam engine, and rechristened her the *Enterprise*. She had "an ugly round nose" that betrayed her past as a stone schooner, and she looked ungainly and slow as she ploughed

The Enterprise, *circa 1890*

through the water. Appearances aside, she did steady but unspectacular business for many years, often serving the smaller lakeshore communities that the more refined and popular vessels could afford to bypass.

After thirteen years in her new role, the *Enterprise* was purchased by Donald W. McDonald, a partner in the Lake Simcoe Transportation and Dry Dock Company, for $500. The ship was refitted once more with an eye towards capturing the tourist trade on Lake Simcoe and in the hope of making her competitive with other steamships operating on the lake. But while the ship was in dry dock it became apparent that her hull was rotting and was likely not up to many more years of service. Construction halted, and in 1897 the ship was sold at public auction to Captain Marsh of Barrie.

Captain Marsh thought he was giving the old vessel

a new lease on life. In reality, she was on life support, kept afloat only by constant repairs and overworked pumps. It was only a matter of time before her aging hull would give in. For several years she sailed to various ports around Lake Simcoe, taking passengers on day cruises and hosting water-borne parties. While hardly lucrative, the *Enterprise* kept busy with Sunday school excursions, creating many fond memories. Fred Jackson reminisced about those days in the *Innisfil Historical Review* of 1951. He remembers how the *Enterprise* sailed Lake Simcoe "…with whistles shrieking and the boat crowded to its capacity, and nearly every mother on board half-frantic when she discovered her boy climbing up the side of the boat from deck to deck and risking a broken neck or a watery grave." Desperate for business, the ship would often pull into a port with brass band playing and offering bargain excursions to "exotic" points around the lake.

It was during one of these day trips in 1903 that the *Enterprise* sprung a leak and began to quickly take on water. Her captain ordered the crew to remain silent so as to not to alarm the passengers, but there was no doubt he was gravely concerned. If the ship were to go down in open water it would be a challenge to get everyone off into the lifeboats without causing a panic that would put lives in jeopardy. Instead, the captain ordered his crew to work the pumps as fast as possible while he used every ounce of his seamanship to nurse the stricken ship back to port. With each passing minute the water in the hold rose and the skipper grew increasingly concerned.

He was relieved when the *Enterprise* limped into Barrie, settling dangerously low in the water. The gangplanks were lowered and the passengers ushered off. No sooner had the last passenger reached the dock, with the crew close on their heels, than the ship sank at the foot of Mulcaster Street. Over the next few days, hundreds of people flocked to the wharves to witness the foundered ship, young Arthur Lower among them.

A week or so later, the *Enterprise* was pumped out and refloated, temporarily patched up, and made ready to sail once again. This, however, was to be her last voyage. She made her way across Lake Simcoe to Jackson's Point without incident, where all her machinery of value was removed. She was then unceremoniously scuttled in the depths of the lake.

For almost a century the *Enterprise* was forgotten, her resting place on the bottom of Lake Simcoe unknown. The vessel's memory was kept alive only through the fictional *Mariposa Belle*, a ship in local author Stephen Leacock's *Sunshine Sketches of a Little Town*, for which she served as inspiration. Then, in 1999, diver William Davidson discovered her watery grave on the bottom of Lake Simcoe. The years had not been kind to the *Enterprise*. The upper hull had collapsed and the side fallen away, leaving only her frame visible. Still, it was a majestic sight and an incredible find. Having witnessed the vandalism of other Lake Simcoe wrecks by recreational divers and fearing the same abuse would befall the *Enterprise,* Davidson has elected to keep the location of the ship a secret.

And so the wreck remains on the bottom, hidden and largely forgotten, a relic of a bygone era that demands our respect and protection as a part of Lake Simcoe's rich heritage.

Chapter 8
A Real Rogue: Joseph Anderton

The Lake Simcoe region was tamed from wilderness, and slowly—over the course of two centuries—developed into one of Ontario's most prosperous areas. It did so on the backs of hardworking and honest settlers, businessmen, elected officials, and entrepreneurs. These productive citizens established the towns and industries, built the roads and schools, and pushed forward the laws and legislature that made Lake Simcoe what it is today.

But there were also men who, though they offered little of substance to the development of the region, certainly added colour to its history. Some of these shady characters were thieves. Others were con men. And then there were disreputable businessmen, who used their wealth and influence to not only solidify their positions in society but also to fleece their fellow man.

Joseph Anderton had the makings of a fine, upstanding businessman, the kind of individual of which the growing town of Barrie could be proud. But there was one problem: he was greedy, conniving, endlessly ambitious, and more than willing to use unsavoury means to acquire power and wealth.

Born in 1830, the son of William Anderton, a local farmer of humble means, he began his life with little in the way of material possessions. Joseph and his brother James were raised in this rustic environment as rugged individualists whose highest credo was self-reliance. They accepted that to achieve success beyond farming they would have to carve a niche for themselves.

The brothers discovered that niche in 1861 when they pooled their resources and established a brewery at the foot of Victoria Street, along the shores of Kempenfelt Bay. Barrie at the time was something of a frontier town and was known for its pie-eyed revelry. It was said that there were more drinking establishments in Barrie than in any comparable-sized town in Ontario. So it should come as no surprise that the Fair View Brewery prospered from the start, and within a year business was so good that expansion was in order. For a time, the brewery was the largest employer in Barrie and dominated the shoreline.

This brewer's paradise attracted other entrepreneurs as well, foremost among them being Robert Simpson. His Simcoe Steam Brewery had previously been located in Kempenfelt and then Tollendal, but fire had chased the businessman from both communities. In 1851, he decided to relocate to Barrie. Business boomed.

A deep rivalry emerged between Joseph Anderton and Robert Simpson. Their competition for business put them at odds, but a deep and mutual personal enmity seemed to form as well. Anderton resented the newcomer's immediate and enviable success, both in business and in politics, and was beside himself when Simpson was elected Barrie's first mayor.

There was more than enough business in this booming market to support several breweries, but Anderton wanted it all for himself. At great expense, in 1868 he purchased the Victoria Hotel, located near Market Square on Collier Sreet. Not only would he make the beer, but now he would also sell it directly to the thirsty populace.

Seven years later, he also added the Queen's Hotel to his holdings. Anderton probably couldn't afford such lavish spending. In December of 1872 his brewery had burned to the ground at a loss of $20,000, only $5,000 of which was covered by insurance. He reopened the following year, borrowing heavily to raise the necessary capital.

What was driving this insatiable appetite for acquisition? After all, many businessmen made a comfortable living with a single hotel or industry. Why put himself so heavily at the mercy of creditors? His spending was driven by greed and envy. As his rival, Simpson, enjoyed greater and greater success, Anderton found himself using less than honourable means of keeping apace. He certainly had no scruples about deceiving people, and the list of individuals whose trust he would come to abuse would read like a who's who of Barrie.

Anderton's greed was eventually his undoing, however. Like Simpson and so many other early industrialists, he had a foot in politics, culminating with his appointment to Mayor of Barrie in 1871. Anderton used his elected position not for the service of the people of his community, but rather to line his own pockets and promote his own self-interest. There was talk, for example, that bribery was used to secure his three-to-one landslide victory over merchant Michael Henry Spencer in the mayoral election.

Despite his political machinations, by 1882 Anderton was heavily in debt, and creditors were nipping at his heels. He figured he could "borrow" $40,000 from the funds of the Barrie Syndicate, money earmarked for the construction of the Canadian Pacific Railway, to make his troubles go away. Unfortunately for Anderton, he was caught in the act when accountants reviewed the books. Anderton had carefully hidden his deception, but not carefully enough.

When the scandal was revealed in March 1883, Anderton left Barrie suddenly and fled to Toronto by rail. As the train drew into the station, the fugitive spotted the police constables making their way through the crowd toward him. His eyes darted frantically about the railcar, looking desperately for a means of escape. His hopes sank when he noticed additional officers standing guard over both entrances.

He was pulled from the train and arrested by the awaiting constables. Anderton was returned to Barrie, where he tried to raise the money he owed by selling the Queen's Hotel, his interests in the brewery, and by mortgaging other properties. At the cost of his entire business empire he managed to pay off most of his outstanding debts.

Incredibly, shortly afterwards, Anderton was re-elected to a seat on the town council. The voters really should have known better. Anderton was soon up to his old tricks again, quietly slipping out of town with about $18,000 in stolen funds and disappearing from the public eye. Joseph Anderton never returned to the scene of his infamy. His reputation has been cleansed with the passage of time so that today he is remembered for being Barrie's first mayor, rather than for being one of its greatest rogues.

As for the Anderton Brewing Company, it carried on quite nicely without its founder. In 1900, the company purchased the rival Simcoe Steam Brewery, some nine years after Robert Simpson's death. Once again, the Anderton Brewing Company held a monopoly over beer production in Barrie, and the brewery prospered like never before. But fire would rear its ugly head and destroy all that been accomplished. On July 9, 1916, the brewery was burnt to the ground. It was never rebuilt. The loss spelled the end of the Anderton beer empire.

At one time, Joseph Anderton was one of Barrie's most eminent businessmen, but in the end he was little more than a common thief. He was never prosecuted for his crimes.

Chapter 9
Murder Most Foul in Morning Glory

What drives someone to take another life? Greed, jealousy, vengeance, hate? Sometimes dark emotions fester for so long that they finally erupt in an explosion of violence. It is difficult for most of us to imagine committing such a heinous act, but murder is very much a part of human history. One infamous murder, the brutal slaying of a woman and her illicit lover in a tiny hamlet just to the south of Lake Simcoe, shamed the entire community.

The hamlet, which once sat between the rural communities of Pefferlaw and Virginia, was known to all who lived there as Morning Glory. The name seemed appropriate: the nearby area was covered in a brilliant sea of flowers that glowed under the bright summer sunshine. A name like Morning Glory suggests a tranquil and peaceful community, and for most of its existence it was. Even in its heyday it would have been a serene setting, surrounded by fields, the silence broken only by the sounds of cattle grazing in the pastures and wagons rambling along the rutted road.

But behind this serene exterior was hidden a dark secret that residents ensured was carefully screened from prying eyes. This secret was kept hidden for nearly a century and only surfaced in the 1950s, when a local school was built and, as the backhoes began excavating soil, the skeletons of two adults were discovered.

The truth was out. Morning Glory, the village that had tried so hard to maintain its idyllic image, had been the scene of a double murder. The news shook the region to its core, and proved that whispered tales were more than rumour. They were the truth.

Morning Glory didn't really have a village core. Instead, its business and homesteads stretched alongside the Sutton Line (today's Highway 48) for a distance of a few kilometres. There were only a few businesses of importance in the community: James Dority ran a small general store, a Mr. Lee owned a brickyard, and there was a sawmill situated on a nearby creek. Keeping the community firmly bonded with faith was Cooke's Presbyterian Church, a humble, rustic frame building that brought the community together every Sunday.

The most notable building in the village was undoubtedly the Morning Glory Tavern, on the site where the Morning Glory Public School now stands. William Sagar was the proprietor, and his establishment was known for its lively environment. It gained a reputation as a place where the liquor flowed fast and cheap, and where drunken brawls were tolerated as a fact of life. Perhaps this was only natural when one considers that most of the clientele consisted of rough-and-ready lumbermen looking for a place to blow off steam.

Mr. Sagar was consumed with his work and the elusive prosperity that was his goal. Running the tavern meant long hours away from his wife, who grew lonely for his company more and more each day. As time passed, Mrs. Sagar started to look elsewhere for the attention she craved. She found it in the arms of a handsome young man. No one knows his identity for certain, but some stories suggest he may have been a labourer or a bartender at the tavern.

Her pulse raced and her blood grew warm when she laid eyes on this young man. She had been so alone for such a long time that when he started to pay Mrs. Sagar the attention she so deeply desired, she found it impossible to resist. As the months passed and her husband's neglect continued, the affair blossomed. Mrs. Sagar's head told her that what she was doing was improper, even sinful, but her heart kept leading her back into the embrace of her new lover.

The busy tavern keeper was oblivious to the affair for a while, but eventually whispered rumours reached his ears and piqued his suspicion. He started to pay more attention to his wife's behaviour, and soon he began to notice that something was amiss. She disappeared for long stretches of time without explanation, she averted her eyes from his gaze, and there seemed to be a youthful bounce in her step. Sure enough, Mr. Sagar also started to notice the lingering looks between his wife and her lover. The rumours were true!

The innkeeper was stunned, hurt, and angry. The more he thought of his wife in the arms of another man the more enraged he became. After all, he worked night and day to provide the necessities of life for her, and this was how she repaid him? His anger simmered for a few days, and slowly he became irrational. Soon, all he could see was the sweet revenge he would have for such betrayal. Overcome with anger, Sagar decided he would catch the two of them in the act and then gain his revenge by killing them both. If his wife and lover wanted to be together so badly, he reasoned, then they would die in each other's arms.

No one knows how and when he did the terrible deed. Did he let them suffer with a slow, tortured death or did he kill them swiftly? Did he enjoy the gratification of killing them with his own hands, perhaps with an axe or knife? Or did he shoot them from across the room? We simply don't know. One way or another, the illicit lovers were dead. After the double murder, Mr. Sagar buried the bodies in the basement of the tavern or somewhere in the yard to cover up his crime. He lied to anyone who would ask about Mrs. Sagar's whereabouts by saying she had run away with another man, and good riddance to her! No one truly believed his story, yet there was not a brave soul in Morning Glory who would try to find out the truth. And so the murder went unpunished.

A dark cloud hovered over the tavern for many years, until it burned to the ground in the early 1880s and was never rebuilt. Most of the residents preferred it that way. It was far easier to forget the shame that marred Morning Glory's good name if the tavern was not there to serve as a constant reminder. In an attempt to put the past behind them, the townspeople never spoke of the murders. It worked. Eventually, the tragic event was virtually wiped from their collective memories. On the rare occasions when an old-timer would try to talk about the event, it was quickly dismissed as nothing more than folklore.

The past is soon forgotten, and the double murder of Mrs. Sagar and her lover would have been lost and buried forever if excavation work in 1957 for the new school hadn't unearthed those grisly remains, much to everyone's surprise and horror.

The past had resurfaced. The story, almost forgotten and long considered nothing more than a tall tale, did not seem so outlandish anymore. The community was forced to confront its past. This peaceful little hamlet, which once took people's breath away with the brilliant colours of its fields, now seemed shrouded in gloom as residents spent long-overdue time mourning two lost lives.

Chapter 10

The Ice Harvest

Throughout the nineteenth century, Lake Simcoe was the driving force behind the prosperity of the communities that grew up along its shoreline.

Some of these communities depended on the bounty of the lake. It sustained a thriving commercial fishery during the summer and North America's largest ice harvesting operation during the winter, when the lake would come alive as men braved the harsh elements and made their way out onto its frozen surface. It was big business, providing winter employment for hundreds of area farmers, and remained an annual tradition for nearly a century. Only fifty years have passed since the last blocks were cut from its frozen surface, and yet today this industry—which made Lake Simcoe known across

Belle Ewart ice workers in 1912

North America—is all but forgotten.

In the nineteenth and first half of the twentieth century, the primary method of refrigeration—vital for the operation of restaurants, hotels, and butchers—came from ice painstakingly cut from countless northern lakes. At the time, Lake Simcoe ice was widely considered to be the best in North America. Tested for purity several times a year, it always achieved a perfect score.

Ice harvesting as an industry began on Lake Simcoe in the 1870s. Rapid shipment to distant markets was important in order to minimize melting in transit, so harvesting was limited to locations where railways came alongside the shoreline and afforded easy loading. The principle areas of operation therefore included Barrie, Jackson's Point, Bell Ewart, and Gilford. Like logging before it, the ice industry provided valuable additional income for area farmers, who offered their services as labourers and hired out their teams of horses to the various ice companies.

Harvesting ice was a time-consuming and laborious procedure, and since work couldn't begin until the lake surface had frozen solid it depended largely upon the whims of nature. Harvesting began in earnest once the ice had reached a thickness of ten to twenty inches, which in a typical year occurred in January or February. There was then a mad dash to bring in the yearly quota before the ice began to melt in March.

The harvesting process began by horses pulling scrapers across the lake's frozen surface in order to smooth it to an acceptable level. Then, the outlines of blocks were marked out with charcoal briquettes. Originally these blocks were cut manually, using handsaws, but by the turn of the century the process became mechanized, with saws driven by steam, and later still, automobile engines. Blocks typically measured 55 by 80 centimetres (22 by 32 inches), and weighed between 20 and 135 kilograms (50 and 300 pounds). They were brought to shore via channels cut into the ice, then deposited in warehouses or directly into waiting railcars by way of a conveyor belt. Sawdust, up to a foot thick, insulated the ice to prevent melting.

Ice from Lake Simcoe was delivered as far away as cities along the eastern seaboard of the United States, some even reaching the Carolinas and Florida. By the time the ice had reached these southerly destinations, however, as much as 40 percent would have melted en route. Because the majority of ice cut on Lake Simcoe was destined for markets in the United States, the industry was dominated by a conglomeration of five American companies called the Ice Union, the largest of its kind in the world. The Ice Union was content to focus on international sales to the metropolises of the American East Coast, leaving the smaller Canadian firms to fulfill local needs. One of these domestic companies was the Lake Simcoe Ice Company.

Originally called the Spring Water Ice Company, the business was formed in Toronto in 1870 by James Fairhead to harvest ice from Lake Wilcox, Bond Lake, and Lake Simcoe. Sales were primarily made to Toronto businesses, but despite the limited market the company flourished. In 1894, Fairhead changed the name of the business to the Lake Simcoe Ice Company in order to capitalize on that lake's reputation for ice purity.

Facilities were located at Jackson's Point and Bell Ewart. The Jackson's Point operation consisted of four large ice houses with a combined capacity of ten thousand tons.

Upward of forty railcars of ice were shipped daily in peak season. Harvesters for the Lake Simcoe Ice Company, who were mostly farmers or summer railhands, earned thirty cents an hour, a very decent wage for the time. The horses employed in the operation were those used in the summer to pull the company's fleet of twenty-five delivery wagons across Toronto.

Another prominent firm involved in the ice industry was the Sarjeant Company of Barrie, well known today as a fuel supplier for Simcoe County. It came as no surprise to anyone when Sarjeant—always a well-diversified business, ever willing to branch out into new areas—began harvesting ice in 1905. Expansion followed, and soon the branch in Orillia was carrying out similar operations on Lake Couchiching. Sarjeant secured a prized contract in 1915, supplying the Buffalo Ice Company in New York State. The company employed between two and three hundred men throughout the winter months.

Other ice companies operated on Lake Simcoe, including the Belle Ewart Ice Company, founded by Alfred Chapman in 1891. Chapman added the 'e' to Bell Ewart, thinking that "Belle" would look more sophisticated on the sides of his Toronto delivery wagons. There was also the Knickerbocker Ice Company, established at Jackson's Point in 1906.

On a smaller scale, many area farmers supplemented their income by cutting, storing, and selling ice to local businesses. They stored the blocks in purpose-built ice houses or remodelled barns lined with bales of hay, and delivered them to area stores and hotels via wagon with the arrival of summer.

Wholesale operations were not the only interested parties behind the ice harvesting. From 1920 until the end of the steam-train era in the 1940s, the Canadian National Railway took a large annual harvest at Allandale (now a part of Barrie) to supply its ice storage facilities all over Ontario, as far away as Kingston and Fort Erie. To facilitate the operation, the CNR built a huge ice-storage depot at Allandale, and a 110-metre (360-foot) platform that allowed up to nine cars to be loaded simultaneously. During the 1920s, the railway cut between 40,000 and 50,000 tons of ice every year.

By this time the industry was in trouble, as artificial ice began to slowly supplant natural ice for most uses. As pure as Lake Simcoe ice may have been, there were inherent drawbacks in harvesting rather than manufacturing ice. Wastage was inevitable during the lengthy shipment by rail; the work of making blocks to fit the iceboxes of the day was time consuming; unseasonably warm winters could undermine profits; and sawdust had to be washed away before delivery in another time-consuming process. Artificial ice was clearly the way forward.

Most companies, seeing what the future had in store, began to wind down their operations, while a few others adopted new technology to remain in business. As early as 1915, for example, the Lake Simcoe Ice Company had built an ice-making plant in Toronto and over the next decade would add three more. By the 1930s, artificial ice was supplying all of its needs. Some companies refused to accept change, but they eventually succumbed to the realities of the industry. In the postwar period, the only company still cutting ice from Lake Simcoe was Barrie Fuel and Supply, which otherwise dealt in coal. The poor harvest of 1949, the result of an extremely mild winter, caused the firm to reconsider its stance and soon it too began making artificial ice.

That decision brought the era of ice harvesting to an end, and a mere sixty years later it is little more than a fading memory. Today, the only people to be found upon the ice on a cold winter's day are the fisherman huddled in his hut and the snowmobiler blazing across its sheer surface. Neither sportsman likely knows anything of the frenzied activity that preceded them upon the frozen surface of Lake Simcoe, nor of its importance to the development of the region.

The Georgina Museum in Sutton boasts some interesting artifacts that reflect back on this forgotten era. On display in the train station are several interesting photos of the local ice-harvesting operations, while tools of the trade, such as pikes and thongs, are found in other buildings. Foremost among these artifacts, however, is a unique ice cutter that demonstrates the ingenious nature of the industry. It consists of an old Ford automobile frame and engine with a large circular saw blade attached to one rear wheel shaft. The saw is on a pivot that allowed the operator to tip the blade in and out of the ice while cutting the blocks.

But these relics belong to the past, as does the industry they served—an industry that briefly made Lake Simcoe known throughout North America. For more than a century, Lake Simcoe enabled numerous industries to develop and thrive, and allowed lakeside communities to flourish. In time, the region moved away from its reliance on the lake to drive its economy, and today Lake Simcoe is used predominantly for play rather than profit. Logging, commercial fishing, the ice industry—all are long gone. But such industries laid the foundation for this vibrant region.

Chapter 11
Otonabee: Lake Simcoe's Last Steamship

The year was 1916. World War I may have been raging in Europe, but that was no reason for Canada's rich and famous to deprive themselves. They continued to flock to the opulent Peninsular Hotel at Big Bay Point, and to enjoy its hospitality. Ontario was, after all, far removed from the realities of a war being fought half a world away. At least it was until that summer.

That is when an explosion aboard Lake Simcoe's "floating palace" brought some of the psychological realities of war to the Barrie area. The blast shattered the morning stillness, breaking windows miles away and sending flames high into the sky. For a few brief moments, people actually thought that their community was under attack, and in those panic-filled moments residents knew the horror faced daily by citizens of the warring states in Europe.

When at last the smoke cleared and the confusion died down, it became clear that there had been no German attack. But a tragedy had occurred all the same, for the explosion had ended the career of a steamship cherished by everyone around Lake Simcoe. On that day in 1916, an icon of the lake died suddenly and dramatically.

The *Otonabee* was one of the last and most luxurious of Lake Simcoe's steamers. But she was also infamous for repeated accidents, malfunctioning equipment, and incompetent piloting, which in later years would tarnish her reputation for elegance and refinement.

From her inaugural appearance on Lake Simcoe, the *Otonabee* was plagued with a poor image. Built in Peterborough, she was dogged by rumours that she was actually an old boat that had been painted over, as a steamer by the same name had sailed the waters of Rice Lake for many years beforehand. Nevertheless, when she made her appearance on Lake Simcoe in 1910, the *Otonabee* was given a clean bill of health. The inspector stated that "the boat was thoroughly sound in every particular, with good engines, and that she would stand any storm on Lake Simcoe."

For the steamer's first cruise someone came up with the unusual idea of sending her up the Holland River to Bradford, despite the fact that no steamer had made the trip in several decades—and for good reason. The Holland River is shallow, and all but the smallest of steamships inevitably found themselves mired in the mud. In addition, Bradford at the time was about as unlikely a tourist destination as one could find on Lake Simcoe, with a few mills and a few dirt streets and absolutely nothing to recommend it. Nevertheless, the cruise went ahead as planned.

The anticipated arrival of the ship, an event unseen hereabouts in a generation, caused a wave of excitement. Throngs of eager spectators, some from as far away as Newmarket and Holland Landing, lined the Bradford shores of the Holland River that day, anxiously awaiting her appearance. For many, it would have been the first time they had seen a steamship up close.

The trip began well enough. The *Otonabee* proved a smooth-sailing vessel as she majestically cut through the waters of Lake Simcoe. But the situation rapidly turned into a farce as she began her voyage up the river. The vessel was simply too deep. Water churned and turned brown with mud, while pike and muskellunge were catapulted through the air in all directions by the struggling paddlewheels. She fought her way along the waterway, dragging her bottom against the

The Otonabee, *circa 1915*

riverbed and several times threatening to get stuck.

Things got no better once the ship reached its destination, either. The town's rotting wharf made landing at Bradford difficult, silt in the river made it difficult to turn the vessel around again, the passengers had to walk into town along railway tracks, and once there they found precious little to see. By any standards, the voyage was a humiliating failure, and yet the passengers and onlookers enjoyed the spectacle immensely.

In 1912, after a few years of carrying passengers to ports around the lake, and including a few return trips to Bradford, the Toronto syndicate that owned the *Otonabee* decided to concentrate her efforts in Kempenfelt Bay. The group owned a new luxury resort at Big Bay Point called the Peninsular Park Hotel, a sixty-room model of luxury and opulence, and they intended the steamer to complement that enterprise. The *Otonabee* spent her days ferrying rich patrons to their accommodations and her nights hosting moonlit cruises upon the lake.

But the *Otonabee* continued to be plagued by ill fortune. Failing engines often left the ship stranded on Kempenfelt Bay, she once crashed into the docks at Big Bay Point, and on another occasion she actually sank at Barrie's dock and had to be refloated and refurbished. The worst accident occurred in 1915, when the *Otonabee* hit the swing bridge at Bosover while ascending the Trent Canal. Her main deck was badly damaged, requiring extensive repairs at great expense. It was hardly worth the effort. She only had one more year to live.

In the predawn gloom of August 14, 1916, the *Otonabee* lay moored at the docks of the Peninsular Hotel. Suddenly, and inexplicably, a fire started below decks. An engineer serving aboard the steamer *Modello*, which also happened to be tied up at the docks, spied the glow of the fire and raced to alert her crew.

He found Captain P. McLean Campbell and purser Harold Hughes asleep aboard the *Otonabee*, and quickly notified them of what by then had become a raging inferno. The hold was already consumed, and flames were licking ravenously at the main deck. With the fire so well established, the officers were powerless to save the ship and had to dive overboard in order to save themselves. Soon, the flames leapt from the ship to the adjacent docks and began racing along the wharf.

"There was a lighthouse at the end of the dock which had several cylinders of gas stored," remembered A. T. Gooch in the *Innisfil Historical Review* for 1954. When the fire gripped hold of this lighthouse and turned it into an over-sized Roman candle, those fighting the fire instantly recognized the danger. At any moment the gas tanks powering the lighthouse's searchlight would ignite and blow up. Mr. Gooch remembered that when the cylinders did finally explode they destroyed the lighthouse, reduced the wharf to splinters, and "broke windows and dishes for quite a distance."

In fact, the sound and reverberations were heard and felt as far away as Barrie. Many people thought the war raging in Europe had somehow come to them, that the Germans had decided to bomb Canada.

It had only been a year since the first air raids were launched by German zeppelins on England. By the summer of 1916, a total of 550 civilians had been killed. Strategic bombing of cities was a terrifying new aspect of war, and even in Canada many people would go to bed wondering if that would be the night bombs fell upon their town.

The explosion at Big Bay Point caused near-hysteria

in some corners. As windows shattered and sent deadly splinters careening into homes, people imagined the worst. Barrie, of course, was well beyond the range of any aircraft of the era. When they were advised of this technical detail, and once the story of the *Otonabee*'s demise emerged, most people calmed down.

As for the ship itself, when the smoke cleared she lay at the bottom of Lake Simcoe, with only her smoke stack showing above the water's surface. Beyond salvage, the burned-out hulk was left for the lake to claim.

Chapter 12
Bradford Convent

During the Victorian era, when Lake Simcoe was booming with economic vitality and its residents were buoyed with optimism and pride, numerous impressive public buildings and private homes rose to demonstrate that their communities were "growing up." Some of these architectural treasures remain today, others were not so fortunate. Even some of the most beautiful and beloved of buildings did not survive, as we see in the tragic story of the Bradford Convent.

There was a time when the town of Bradford had a castle on the hill. It was not the home of kings or queens, but still, those living within this elegant mansion were among the community's wealthiest and most influential individuals. At its most majestic the manor reflected Bradford's heyday, a

Bradford Convent, circa 1900

brief era when the town enjoyed a prominence never experienced before or since.

The building that much later became known as the Convent was built in 1876 as the home of John MacLean Stevenson, a clerk of the Simcoe County Court from 1877 to 1906. The late 1870s through to the 1890s saw Bradford's growth as a commercial centre, specifically as a terminus for shipping grain via rail. Many of the homes built at this time reflected this prosperity, and Stevenson's was no different. The two-storey brick home was built on a grand scale in the "Italianate style," with impressive, high-ceilinged rooms and a tall, centrally located "campanile," or bell tower. Its location on a rise of land overlooking Bradford and the broad Holland Marsh below gave it a decided dominance, and the view from the tower was breathtaking and unequalled in town.

Stevenson owned the home for less than a year before selling it to Robert Bingham. The Bingham family was conventional enough in origin. Robert was born in 1814, the son of recent English immigrants. His wealth was based on local hotel interests, which by the late nineteenth century were flourishing so well that Robert could afford to purchase a fine house. Bingham, in light of the stunning vistas visible from the upper windows, named the house "Fairview."

Robert Bingham passed away in his bed on April 14, 1892, at the age of seventy-eight. Fairview then passed to his daughter Emily and her husband, James Boddy. James was a well-to-do merchant who had inherited a store from his father, John Boddy, and who would later (in 1896) become Warden of Simcoe County. The Boddys only remained in Bradford for another decade before moving their business to Hamilton in 1903. Fairview then passed into the possession of Reverend Egerton R. Young, Robert Bingham's brother-in-law through his sister Elizabeth.

Reverend Young had led something of a colorful life. Born in Smith's Falls in 1840, the son of a Methodist minister, he taught school until the age of twenty-three, when he followed his father into the clergy. From 1868 to 1876 Reverend

Young was a missionary among the Cree and Ojibwa Indians of Northern Manitoba and was called upon to settle grievances between them and the Federal Government. He was instrumental in averting armed conflict on several occasions. After returning home Reverend Young spent the remainder of his years lecturing and writing extensively about his experiences in the West. Inspired by the wilds, he re-christened the house "Algonquin Lodge." When Egerton Young died peacefully in bed in 1909, Algonquin Lodge was purchased by Samuel Lukes. The manor subsequently became known simply as "The Lukes House."

The Lukes family was prominent both in Bradford and Newmarket. Samuel's father, John Lukes, was considered the finest master miller in Newmarket, and his brother William erected Lukes' Grist Mill on Huron Street in Newmarket in 1876. For his part Samuel built the Bradford Flour Mill in 1878, which flourished as Bradford's role in the grain industry expanded. It was his mill that processed local grain, the product of dozens of area farms, in preparation for shipment by train to distant markets.

The Bradford Flour Mill was one of the largest and most productive in Ontario. It was only the third flourmill in the province to be equipped with the then-cutting-edge roller system for grinding grain. It boosted efficiency so much that the mill produced more than two hundred barrels of flour a day. To keep up with the demand, Lukes employed twelve men and kept the mill humming day and night for almost eight months of the year.

The business grew in leaps and bounds. He had ready markets in Toronto, Montreal, Quebec City, and even as far away as England. Local farmers could no longer supply all his needs, so he began purchasing premium grain from Manitoba. In 1904 newly installed machinery boosted capacity again to three hundred barrels of flour per day.

But despite Samuel Lukes' success in business, personal tragedy stalked him. In a five-year span, he lost three infant children. Daniel Lukes, aged seven months, died of "diarrhea" in 1888; William Bailey Lukes, aged ten months, died from "summer complaint" in 1889; and Helen Lukes, also aged ten months, died of "congestion of the brain" in 1893. Lukes was virtually inconsolable over his children's deaths. He tried to assuage his grief by working from dawn to dusk in the mill. As a result the business prospered as never before, and Lukes became extremely wealthy. It was this affluence that allowed him to purchase "Algonquin Lodge" in 1909 and make many improvements. With no expense spared, it became the ultimate in opulence in Bradford. Lukes ensured his home was as modern as possible, with electric lighting and hot water, the first in Bradford to have such luxuries.

The Lukes were thrilled with their new home. Samuel's wife loved to entertain, hosting extravagant parties for the town's wealthiest citizens in the Lukes' own ballroom. Samuel himself could not remember ever being happier. It was a magical time for the family, living in such an enchanting home.

The fairy-tale existence could not last forever. The mill burned down in 1923, and in 1949, after seventy-three years as a private residence and forty years in the Lukes family, the then-abandoned Algonquin Lodge was sold to a Catholic order of nuns known as the Ursuline Order. The building was not merely a residence for the Sisters. Under their direction it became a Catholic all-girls' school, noted locally for academic excellence. Two generations of Bradford's young ladies were educated by the sisters and taught how to behave as the Lord expects.

Twenty years later, the convent was uninhabited once more. In 1969, Bradford resident John Moniz purchased the building and converted it into four rental apartments. Sadly, the years were not kind to the majestic building. Neglected, it slowly ran to ruin. By 1994, when it was assumed by the Town of Bradford–West Gwillimbury, the building was silent, forlorn, and weary with age. Despite ambitious proposals to renovate the structure and put it to use in a new capacity, the town elected to resolve the issue with a bulldozer. The demolition was a tragic ending that pained many in town.

The convent was an unmistakable sight in late nineteenth- and twentieth-century Bradford. It was probably the most recognizable building in town, and through it the pulse of Victorian and Edwardian Bradford continued to beat. When it was demolished, not only was a grand building destroyed—so too were the town's ties to the past.

Chapter 13
Resort Country

Some of Lake Simcoe's industries depended not on the bounty of the water, but rather its beauty. From the 1880s through the early twentieth century, the pristine waters drew tourists by the thousands, supporting resorts and sightseeing excursions aboard steamships.

Today, Muskoka is known as "Cottage Country," Ontario's undisputed favourite vacation destination, famed for relaxation, tranquility, and an abundance of trees, water, and wildlife. But for a time Muskoka had a rival for that title: Lake Simcoe, which boasted its own share of wilderness, water, and welcoming resorts.

The region's rise as a vacationer's paradise began in the late 1800s, when farmers whose properties bordered the lake

The Peninsular Hotel, circa 1910

realized they could earn extra income by converting their shorelines into picnic grounds and campsites. Word soon spread about the beautiful waters and the placid setting, and demand grew. To accommodate their guests, campgrounds expanded their operations with rented summer cottages and, in some cases, seasonal resorts. It was not long before Lake Simcoe was attracting guests from as far afield as the eastern United States. The breathtaking scenery, pristine lake, calming serenity, and clean, invigorating air gave city dwellers a chance to escape not only the heat of summer but also the congestion and pressures of business.

An entire industry grew up, catering to these wealthy

Couchiching Hotel in 1877

summer visitors. Boatbuilders rented boats to guests for fishing and leisurely rows on the lake, steamers scheduled sightseeing cruises and midnight excursions, farmers sold their finest fresh produce to local resorts, and seasonal businesses emerged. Tourism around Lake Simcoe flourished, and it did so just as other industries that had long sustained the region—notably lumbering and commercial fishing—were on their last legs.

The first resort to appear was the grandest, but also one of the shortest-lived: the Couchiching Hotel. By 1871 the residents of Orillia were uncomfortably aware that they were beginning to lag behind other Simcoe County towns, most notably Barrie, in terms of prosperity. The arrival of the

Northern Railway seemed to offer a chance to reverse that situation: it was now easier than ever for people to visit Orillia and take in the charms of picturesque Lake Couchiching. If only there was a resort in which to accommodate guests, surely tourism would take off.

Calculating that it would line its shareholders' pockets with gold, the Northern Railway decided to fill this void. The site it had in mind was Steamboat Point, on the north end of the Narrows that separated Lake Simcoe and Lake Couchiching. It was a beautiful piece of land, offering unparalleled views of the lake and quiet solitude removed from the bustle of town.

Built between 1872 and 1873 for the almost unheard of sum of $75,000, the Couchiching Hotel was the grandest resort ever seen on lakes Simcoe or Couchiching, and to that date one of the finest anywhere in Ontario. A graceful lane leading through trees greeted passengers as they stepped off the train. Walking towards the main building, visitors would have marvelled at the surrounding 180-acre park, filled with flowerbeds, manicured lawns, croquet greens, elegant pavilions, and shaded paths.

The hotel itself accommodated four hundred guests in refined style and gracious gentility. Guestrooms were charmingly furnished and had panoramic views overlooking the water; the grand dining room offered meals second to none in a relaxed atmosphere; and there was a billiard hall and bar where gentlemen could relax. The most unusual feature was undoubtedly the carbide gas light fixtures, a very modern convenience that was almost unheard of in that day and age.

The Couchiching Hotel was certainly a sight to behold, a destination in its own right. Reaping the rewards from an advertising campaign throughout North America and England, during its first summer it was fully booked. Guests that first year included Canada's Governor-General, Lord Dufferin and his wife; General McClelland and a host of other officers of American Civil War fame; Lieutenant-Governor D. A. McDonald; and Ontario's premier, Oliver Mowat.

From the start the Couchiching Hotel was a spectacular success, but unfortunately that success was fleeting. In October 1876, after only three seasons in operation, the impressive resort was destroyed by fire when flames escaped from a defective flue in the reading room and quickly raced throughout the all-wood structure. Only the outbuildings, such as the servants' quarters and the "fishing temple" overlooking the lake, were saved from the inferno. Insurance covered only $36,000-worth of the damage.

By this time the Northern Railway was already pushing onward into the stunning wilds of Muskoka, a region even better suited for luxury resorts, and consequently the resort's owners did not rebuild the Couchiching Hotel. Hope died hard, however, especially since the community's economic well-being was at stake. A group of eighteen local businessmen approached the Orillia town council for a $10,000 loan to rebuild the hotel themselves, but were ultimately turned down. All further attempts at raising finance also failed and the group finally had to concede defeat.

The Couchiching Hotel's status as the grandest resort on the lake was assumed by the Peninsular Hotel, located on the tip of Big Bay Point, near Barrie. At one time one of the finest seasonal resorts in Canada, it was a place where the rich and famous came to relax and unwind. For almost seventy-five years its reputation for comfort and hospitality, an oasis of refinement, was nearly unmatched.

For most of the nineteenth century, Big Bay Point had been covered in forests and was home to only a few scattered farms. That changed suddenly in 1887 when the new hotel, the dream of G. C. Power and a group of Barrie investors, opened in the summer of 1887. The finely appointed resort featured sixty guestrooms, many with views overlooking the placid waters of Lake Simcoe, a beautiful shaded veranda that surrounded the entire building, and an elegant dining room capable of accommodating more than a hundred people.

Almost immediately, the Peninsular Hotel became a hit among Americans curious for a glimpse of the "wilds of Canada." By the turn of the century it had become arguably the most fashionable summer resort in Ontario, and among the finest in Canada. The hotel was the favoured vacation destination of Sir Wilfred Laurier during his term as Prime

Minister, and numerous prominent Toronto businessmen shared his affinity for the resort's combination of elegance and tranquility. Many stayed all summer, and some eventually bought cottages of their own in the area.

But after only a few decades the Peninsular Hotel saw a notable decline in its popularity. The period from 1910 through the 1930s was particularly hard on the resort. A combination of circumstances all undermined the hotel's profitability and previous reputation for excellence. New resorts in Muskoka lured vacationers away. Business was interrupted by World War I between 1914 and 1918, followed by the onset of the Depression in 1929. And finally, the aging facilities were badly in need of repair.

A reversal of fortune occurred in 1933 when Cecil Grant, a bright entrepreneur with extensive experience in the hospitality industry, purchased the aging resort. He believed the Peninsular Hotel still had some life in it. After extensive renovation and redecoration it was reopened as the Big Bay Point Hotel.

The excitement generated by the re-invention was electric, and returning vacationers brought a renewed sense of optimism. "The large frame building with its wide verandahs...is one of the most comfortable and attractive summer inns around Lake District," noted the *Barrie Northern Advance* on July 4, 1935. Later that same season, the paper reported that "the beautiful walks, trees and grounds and opportunities for riding and tennis around the Big Bay Point Hotel helped attract many visitors, to say nothing of the comfort to be had within." It seemed as if the glory days had returned.

Grant operated Big Bay Point Hotel successfully and profitably until 1950, at which point it was sold to local interests. Despite the change of ownership, business carried on much as before for several years. Unfortunately, the resort would never open for the 1955 season, which would have been its sixty-seventh.

In the early evening of April 9 a fire started in a small building at the rear of the hotel. Joint efforts by the Barrie and Innisfil fire departments to prevent the flames from spreading to the main building were in vain, and soon the all-wood structure was completely engulfed. By midnight, the once-lavish hotel had been reduced to ash and glowing embers. All that could be saved were some dining-room furniture, a piano, and some linen. The destruction was complete, the loss staggering. Big Bay Point Hotel was never rebuilt.

The Couchiching and Big Bay Point hotels were not the only Lake Simcoe resorts that were claimed by fire. Beaverton's Victoria Park Hotel was razed in 1929 after several decades of providing warm memories for countless summer guests, many of whom returned year after year.

The Island House on Strawberry Island suffered an equally tragic fate. Built in the 1880s by Charles McInnes, a former Great Lakes shipmaster who spared no expense in its construction, the hotel was beautiful and enjoyed a decade of prosperity. The hotel experienced some lean years after the turn of the century, but McInnes was a tireless promoter, boundlessly enthusiastic, and somehow always managed to make ends meet. When McInnes died of Bright's Disease in 1913, Island House never again saw a guest.

For every resort that had a spectacular end, there were two that simply faded away: Rotherwood, Jackson's Point Hotel, Robinson House, Simcoe House, Jackson Villa, and others. Tourism trends were changing. In the face of all their challenges Lake Simcoe's resorts found themselves hard-pressed to remain in business. Many closed, though a few struggled on for a number of years before it became painfully obvious that most tourists were not going to return, and those that did preferred to own cottages rather than stay at a hotel. By the 1920s the heyday of Lake Simcoe's resort era was over.

Ironically, it was around this time that the only resort still existing today—the Briars Resort and Spa of Georgina—began to emerge as a tourist destination. The story of this famed and heritage-rich property is told in the next chapter. It carries on the legacy of Lake Simcoe's elegant summer hotels in fine style, a reminder that at one time Lake Simcoe was indeed "Cottage Country."

Chapter 14

The Briars Resort and Spa

There was a time not so long ago when a vacation at a northern resort meant a stay at a family-run property. The owners were also the hosts, and they knew all the guests by name. You were welcomed as one of the family, and were warmly invited to return, year after year. Times have changed. Resorts today are run by the impersonal hand of corporations. The intimate one-on-one connection between host and guest, the comfortable home-like feeling, the warmth of hospitality that makes you want to return over and over again—these civilities seem all but forgotten at modern resorts.

One place that does manage to capture these timeless

qualities is The Briars Resort and Spa, located on the shores of Lake Simcoe near Sutton. Beyond being popular, The Briars is a property of immense historical significance. For almost 150 years The Briars, and the Sibbald family who have owned it for multiple generations, has had a profound impact on the region.

To say that the estate is rich in history is a gross under-statement. The Briars story begins in 1840 when Captain William Bourchier, a retired Royal Navy officer, arrived in Georgina with his wife and settled on land given him by a grateful British government for decades of dutiful service. When it came time to choosing a design for his new home, Bourchier's mind went back to a delightful manor in which he had previously stayed: a graceful home on the British island of Saint Helena called The Briars. It was a manor that had been the home-in-exile of the deposed French Emperor Napoleon Bonaparte. The captain borrowed the design, and what's more, he borrowed the name.

Bourchier built his elegant mansion the same year that he arrived, and it was the marvel of the region, looming in size and opulence over the humble settler cottages that dominated the area. Its situation was chosen to enjoy the best view of the blue expanse of Lake Simcoe. Unfortunately, Captain Bourchier did not get to enjoy the vista for long, dying suddenly in 1844. His widow didn't seem to enjoy The Briars as much as he had, and only stayed there rarely.

The Briars Resort and Spa today

Eventually, the property was put up for sale.

In 1872, the manor was purchased by Doctor Francis (Frank) Sibbald, the eighth son of Susan Sibbald, an aristocratic woman whom we met in Chapter 3, and who owned nearby Eldon Hall, the centrepiece of modern-day Sibbald Point Provincial Park. A former army physician and a medical missionary in Shanghai, and the product of a wealthy family, Doctor Sibbald wanted a fine home in which to spend his retirement years. He also wanted a property that he could turn into a working estate farm. The Briars matched his needs perfectly.

Frank immediately put his stamp on The Briars, and

many of the buildings he erected remain today, though they no longer serve their original roles. He added a brick coach house (now part of the dining room) and a bell tower that was used as a clock for workers on the farm. He expanded the home to include a service wing and a summer wing with two drawing rooms. Many of the rooms in these additions serve as Heritage guest rooms. In addition he erected a barn that later served as home of the Red Barn Theatre, until it was razed by a tragic fire in 2009. The most unusual feature was a peacock house, which he went to great lengths to fill with peacocks imported from India. The peacock house is unique in the province and has been designated a structure of historic importance by Ontario Heritage.

Frank Sibbald was a sociable man and a gracious host. He delighted in holding garden parties and church socials at The Briars, and often as many as five hundred guests from all over Georgina would attend. Many of these parties were held in the driveway between the home and the coach house. Many modern guests sit down for dinner on the very spot where Frank's guests would have done so more than a century earlier, as the modern dining room encompasses the driveway.

When Frank died unmarried in 1904, the Briars passed to his niece, Elizabeth Kemp Sibbald, who in turn left it to Frank Drinkwater Sibbald, also known as Jack. It was Jack Sibbald who first directed the Briars toward the hospitality industry

A party at The Briars, circa 1890

when, around 1940, he began renting out cottages on the lake to friends who wished to enjoy the estate's peacefulness during the summer months. Word about the property's charms soon spread, and as it did so, demand for cottages and the need for enhanced services for the paying guests grew. In 1942 a cook and a few local girls were hired to wait on tables and keep house. The Briars Resort was beginning to take shape.

The past seventy years have seen countless changes at The Briars. It has evolved from an impromptu summer cottage retreat to a full-scale modern resort with all the latest amenities. Seeing it all develop over the years, and guiding the resort's evolution, is current owner John Sibbald. John initially had no intention of joining his father and making operating the resort his career. With an engineering degree, he had other plans. His father eventually won him over, but John agreed only on the condition that he could make the changes he deemed necessary for modernizing the business.

In 1977 extensive renovations were made to the Briars and the resort opened for its first winter, making it a four-season resort. John was also one of the first resort owners in Ontario to embrace business conventions, which he recognized were vital to making the resort profitable and sustainable year round. The Briars now features an indoor swimming pool, a spa, and a variety of other luxurious amenities that guests during the 1940s couldn't even dream of.

That's the story of The Briars so often told to guests and written about in books and periodicals. But that's only one side of the story. There are countless secrets: important architectural details, fascinating historical tidbits, priceless family memories that most people are never privy to. Many of these came to the surface while we toured the property with John Sibbald, who continues to runs The Briars alongside his wife, Barbara, and their sons, Hugh and Andrew. As we walked alongside him down memory lane, we discovered a loving family man who was willing to share the most personal memories with us. It was not long before the engrossing history of The Briars and the Sibbald family that calls it home unfolded.

John Sibbald began our tour in the dining room. "Can you believe this was the original carriage house and stables?" he asks, pointing to a private function room accessed through a pair of barn-like double-doors. The four stone pillars within the room, we learn, were once the base of the 60-foot tall bell tower. By the 1950s the tower began to rot and sway in the wind, so had to be torn down. The bell, however, survived and now stands in a smaller tower on the property.

We were still trying to picture this elegant restaurant as a carriage house and driveway, when John excitedly led us on to something else that has jogged his memory. "This chandelier came from Casa Loma in Toronto. My family bought it at auction after Casa Loma's builder, Sir Henry Pellatt, went bankrupt. Some of the wall sconces are from Casa Loma as well." We marvelled at the ornate fixtures, appreciating them for the historic artifacts that they were. We began to realize that even simple furnishings or décor at The Briars, things most guests wouldn't even take notice of, had a story behind them.

John then slowly led us through the original 1840 manor house which held countless memories; he grew up within its rustic rooms, and for many years conducted business affairs from an upper-floor office. John pointed out the summer wing added by Frank Sibbald in 1880 and identified every room as they were originally employed a century ago: kitchen and servant quarters in the basement, dining room and salon on the main floor, bedrooms upstairs. Every fireplace dates back to the time of construction and represented the only source of heat in the building until the mid-1900s.

A faraway look appeared in John's eyes as he remembered that his mother was great at hosting social gatherings, just as Frank Sibbald was before her. "Mother would have these tea parties once a week and the ladies would bring their daughters. She loved hosting parties." A smile spread across his face at that point. "I remember tying the girls under the tables so I wouldn't have to play with them."

The Briars still has gatherings for their guests, carrying on a tradition dating back more than a hundred years. Although they no longer attract up to 700 people, as Frank Sibbald's strawberry socials did in the 1890s and 1880s, they remain the highlight of the resort's social calendar and are loved by staff and guests alike. Intimate touches make them magical events, feeling more like family gatherings than an event put on for strangers. Every Christmas Eve, for example, John Sibbald's very first story book, *Twas the Night Before Christmas*, is brought out from the Heritage Room (what is essentially a museum of Sibbald history) and read for the assembled guests.

Another of John's prized possessions is an autographed picture of famed Canadian author Mazo de la Roche (author of the beloved *Jalna* series), which hangs in the library within the old manor house. John remembers Mazo de la Roche well; she was a regular guest and was one of his favorite people. Mazo de la Roche wrote several of her books while staying in Cottage Two at the Briars, and the resort was an influence on her work, appearing in form if not name in several of her books. She spent her last five summers at The Briars, and it's only fitting that when she died, she was buried at nearby St. George's Cemetery where generations of the Sibbalds have been interned.

The grounds outside are equally rich with history, memories, and tradition. Many of the non-native trees, as well as the hedges lining Hedge Road, are rare in Ontario and were planted by Frank Sibbald back in the nineteenth century. Other trees on-site are hundreds of years old, some dating back to the 1600s and may have stood when French explorer Samuel de Champlain first visited Lake Simcoe. For these reasons, the Arboretum at the University of Guelph has recognized The Briars for its natural and arboricultural heritage.

At the end of our tour, we came upon an authentic suit of samurai armour near the entrance to Drinkwaters Lounge. The armour had been purchased by Frank Sibbald on one of his many trips to Japan while practicing medicine during the period 1845–1875, and has been a treasured family heirloom ever since. As we stood in front of the armour and admired its artistry, John started to laugh and shared one final memory of what must have been a joyous youth. "I recall dressing up in it once. I must have been about fourteen years old... it was the kind of thing I would do to get a reaction out of people. There was a woman guest who came every year and was very nervous. I decided to put the armour on in the middle of the night and walk up and down the halls to scare her." A broad smile stretches across his face. "It worked, too!"

The Briars has changed a lot since it was built in 1840, and most especially since it was transformed into a resort some seventy years ago. What remains consistent, however, is the Sibbald family's warmth and genuine hospitality.

Acknowledgments

A book such as this is built as much on the generosity of others as it is on the passion of the writers. Many individuals over the years have shaped our knowledge of and enthusiasm for the fascinating story that is Lake Simcoe's history, and while we cannot acknowledge or even remember them all we are nonetheless profoundly grateful to each.

But some people must be thanked publicly for their concrete and invaluable assistance in putting *Secrets of Lake Simcoe* together. Foremost among these are the Sibbald family of The Briars Resort, who generously opened their doors and their memories to us. Their love for the Lake Simcoe region was very much the spark that inspired this book, so while only a chapter is devoted to the Sibbalds and their timeless resort, their spirit can be felt throughout the book's entirety.

In addition, we'd like to point out the kind assistance of Philip Rose Donohue, curator of Georgina Pioneer Village and Archives; Debra Mann and Mandy Pethick of the Innisfil Public Library; and Bruce Beacock at the Simcoe County Archives. Thanks also go out to Nancy Sewell at James Lorimer for seeing the potential in this book, and for her support and understanding during the writing process.

Writing books is a cooperative effort between Maria

and me, so it goes without saying that I thank Maria for her contribution with each new book we write. But in this case, I must extend a special note of appreciation because she took on the journey that is writing a book in spite of hardships in her own life. Maria is the strongest person I know and, as this manuscript leaves our hands, I find myself respecting her more than ever.

Andrew Hind

Photographic Credits

The watercolour on the cover of this book, "J. C. Morrison" by Duncan Macpherson, is reproduced by permission of Dorothy Macpherson.

Photographs on the following pages appear courtesy of the following sources:

p. 20, Andrew Hind; p. 35, Georgina Pioneer Village and Archives; p. 41, Diana Robichaud; p. 59, Parry Sound Public Library; p. 66, Georgina Pioneer Village and Archives; p. 83, Innisfil Historical Society and Innisfil Public Library; p. 93, Innisfil Historical Society; p. 98, Bradford Public Library; p. 105, Innisfil Historical Society; p. 106, Simcoe County Archives; p. 115, Peter Sibbald and The Briars Resort and Spa; p. 117, The Briars Resort and Spa.

Bibliography

Berchem, F. R. *The Yonge Street Story, 1793–1860*. Toronto: McGraw-Hill Ryerson, 1977.

Byers, Mary. *Lake Simcoe and Lake Couchiching*. Erin, Ontario: Boston Mills Press, 1999.

Hopkins, Jeanne. *Jackson's Point: Ontario's First Cottage Country*. Erin, Ontario: Boston Mills Press, 1993.

Hunter, Andrew F. *The History of Simcoe County*. Barrie: Historical Committee of Simcoe County, 1909.

____. *Lake Simcoe and Its Environs*. Barrie: Barrie Examiner, 1893.

Illustrated Historical Atlas of York County. Toronto: Miles and Co., 1878.

Innisfil Historical Society. *The Ice Industry of Belle Ewart*. Stroud, Ontario: Innisfil Historical Society, 1982.

Jury, Wilfred. *The Nine Mile Portage from Kempenfelt Bay to the Nottawasaga River*. London, Ontario: Museum of Indian Archaeology, University of Western Ontario, 1956.

Murdoch, Sue and B. E. S. Rudachyk. *Beautiful Barrie: The City and Its People*. Barrie, ON: Barrie Press Inc., 2005.

Williamson, Scott. *"Historical Shipwreck Found in Lake Simcoe,"* The Lake Simcoe Marine Heritage Society. November, 2000.

About the Authors

Andrew Hind is a freelance writer who lives in Bradford, Ontario. His feature articles have appeared in magazines and newspapers across Canada, in the United States, and in England. Andrew developed a passion for history early on, especially for unusual and obscure events that are typically overlooked or quickly forgotten. He hopes, through his writing, to bring these fascinating stories to light for a modern audience.

Maria da Silva has always had a passion for history and ghost stories. Though she came from a country (Portugal) that is full of history and the unknown, she never dreamed that her future would lead her into writing about the forgotten and the unexplained. Maria's work, co-authored with Andrew Hind, has appeared in publications such as *Fate* and *Mystery Magazine*.

Index

Lake Ontario and
   Georgian Bay Canal
   (*see also* Ghost Canal,
   The), 44-45
Lake Simcoe Ice
   Company, 85, 88
Laughton, William,
   53-55
Laurier, Sir Wilfred, 42,
   48, 109
Lee, Captain Simon,
   36-37
Lower, Arthur, 64, 68
Lukes, Samuel, 100-102

M
Maitland, Sir Peregrine,
   14, 15
Matilda, *59*, 59-63
McDonald, Donald
   W., 66
McInnes, Charles,
   111-12
McPherson, James, 65
Morning, 50, 52, 53-57
Morning Glory, 76-81
Mulock, William, 42,
   45-48, 49
Muskoka, 11, 104, 108,
   110

N
Newmarket, 41, 44, 45,
   46, 47, 48, 100
Newmarket Canal (*see
   also* Ghost Canal),
   45-48
Nine Mile Portage,
   20-22, 24-26
Northern Railway,
   55-56, 107, 108
North West Company,
   13

O
Orillia, 35, 54, 60, 86,

106-107, 109
Otonabee, 52, 91-96, *93*

P
Pefferlaw, 76
Penetanguishene, 31
Peninsular Hotel (*see
   also* Big Bay Point
   Hotel), 90, 94, *105*,
   109-10
Perry, Oliver Hazard, 21

R
Rains, William
   Kingdom, 28-33
Ready, Mary, 36-38
Roches Point, 15, 56
Rogers Reservoir, 16, 49

S
Sagar, William, 78-80
Sibbald, Charles, 34, 35
Sibbald, Francis
   (Frank), 115-16, 119,
   120, 121
Sibbald, Frank
   Drinkwater (Jack),
   116-17
Sibbald, John, 118-22
Sibbald Point Provincial
   Park, 16, 31, 36, 115
Sibbald, Susan, 31,
   34-36, 37-38, 115
Sibbald, William, 34, 35,
   36-39
Simcoe, John Graves, 13
Simcoe Steam Brewery,
   72, 74
Simpson, Robert, 72, 73
Sir John Colborne, 52,
   53
Soules, David, 25-26
Stevenson, John
   MacLean, 98-99
St. Joseph Island, 31-33
Sutton, 33, 61, 88, 113

T
Thompson,
   Charles Poulett
   ("Steamboat"), 52-55,
   56-57
Thompson, Sir John, 24
Tollendal, 72
tourism, 15, 16, 104-106
Trent-Severn Waterway,
   40, 42

V
Victoria Park Hotel, 111
Virginia, ON, 76

W
War of 1812, 11, 13, 19,
   20, 21-24
Willow Creek, 21, 22
Woodbridge, 43
World War I, 90-91, 95,
   110

Y
Young, Reverend
   Egerton R., 99-100